Park Hill, Westmoreland
1762

COLONIAL MEETING-HOUSES
of New Hampshire

Compared with their Contemporaries
in New England

---

by

E V A A. S P E A R E

Published under the Auspices of

DAUGHTERS OF COLONIAL WARS

State of New Hampshire

Copyright, 1938
by
EVA A. SPEARE

PRINTED IN THE UNITED STATES OF AMERICA
BY THE COURIER PRINTING COMPANY
LITTLETON, N. H.

INTRODUCTION

A casual incident often induces an absorbing hobby. Thus during an afternoon drive several historically minded individuals fortuitously decided to explore the State of New Hampshire in search of its colonial meeting-houses. Gradually this quest extended into a pilgrimage into distant sections of New England. Meanwhile their friends facetiously christened the group, The Explorers.

Not until November of 1932 did this hobby attain its maximum pace. Nature propitiously prolonged the Indian's summer. Unbelievable in this northern climate is the fact that on the first of December the explorers enjoyed a picnic on New Durham Ridge sitting upon dry leaves beneath an oak, wearing no top-coats and gazing at the panorama of peaks of the White Mountains on the far horizon through a haze as blue as that of an August afternoon. The lunch basket, always supplemented by a thermos of hot bisque and another of steaming coffee, was a source of pleasure on those autumn trips.

The group consisted of an experienced photographer whose camera functioned even in the dim light of an attic, a skilled woman-chauffeur, a scribe with an inquisitive eye and several companions whose interest fluctuated between amused curiosity or unconcealed boredom if the antiquarians prolonged the expeditions into late afternoon rambles.

When the winter season prevented further explorations, the perusal of town histories and volumes about colonial architecture occupied many leisure hours. At length the results of this research has been recorded with the purpose of expressing appreciation by their beneficiaries of a legacy from preceding centuries, a priceless heritage for generations yet unborn.

CONTENTS

INTRODUCTION V

CONTENTS VII

LIST OF ILLUSTRATIONS IX

LIST OF MEETING-HOUSES IN NEW HAMPSHIRE XIV

CHAPTERS

I THE TOWN MEETING-HOUSE 1

II THE MEETING-HOUSE AT SANDOWN 7

III BUILDING A MEETING-HOUSE 22

IV EARLY MEETING-HOUSES WITHOUT STEEPLES 35

V THE EARLIEST TOWNSHIPS 48

VI THE EASTSIDE MEETING-HOUSES 61

VII BETWEEN THE RIVER VALLEYS 71

VIII EARLY STEEPLES AND THEIR BELLS 89

IX STORIED STEEPLES 105

X THE ANGLICAN CHURCH IN THE COLONY 159

XI QUAKERS IN NEW HAMPSHIRE 175

XII BEYOND NEW HAMPSHIRE 181

XIII THE INFLUENCE OF CHARLES BULFINCH 211

ACKNOWLEDGMENTS 234

BIBLIOGRAPHY 235

INDEX 236

ILLUSTRATIONS

Park Hill, Westmoreland   *Frontispiece*

The Second Meeting-house in Concord   XVI
  Federal Constitution ratified here, 1788.

The Alexander Studio, MacDowell Colony, Peterborough   4

The Ancient Cemetery, East Derry   5

The Hill-top at Sandown   6

The Town Pound, Sandown   8

The Rear Windows, Sandown   9

The South Doorway, Sandown   10

The Goblet Pulpit, Sandown   12

The Staircase of the Goblet Pulpit, Sandown   14

The Sacred Desk, Sandown   16

The Front Seat of Honor and Square Pews, Sandown   18

The Front Balcony, Sandown   19

The Frame in the Attic, Sandown   20

The Log Meeting-house at Penny Cook, now Concord   22

The Congregational Church at Amherst   24

The King Post Trusses, Sandown   28

The Meeting-house at North Danville   34

The Sounding Board of the Oldest Pulpit, North Danville   36

The Choir Stall at Fremont   38

The Meeting-house at Fremont   40

The Meeting-house at Allenstown   42

The Interior at Allenstown   43

The Smith Corner Meeting-house at Gilmanton   45

The Dana Hill Meeting-house at New Hampton   46

The Site of the Fort Meeting-house at Dover Point   50

The Oldest Meeting-house at Newington   51

The Town Horse Block at Newington   54

The Present Pulpit at Newington   55

The Meeting-house at Exeter, now Congregational Church   56

The North Meeting-house at Portsmouth in 1712   59
Where George Washington attended a service, 1789.

The Church at Newcastle, Bulfinch Design   60

Barnstead Parade   62

The Choir Stall at Leighton's Corner   65

The Meeting-house at Wakefield, now Congregational Church   66

The Meeting-house at Effingham   68

Ordination Rock at Tamworth   70

The Meeting-house at Hopkinton, now Congregational Church   72

The Town-house at Washington   76

Interior, the Gallery Posts at Washington   77

The Church at Stoddard   78

The Town-house at Lempster   79

The Meeting House at North Sutton   81

Canaan Street and Town-house   82

A Bier in Bradford, The Pond Meeting-house   84

The South Road Meeting-house at Salisbury   86

The Meeting-house at Hebron, now Congregational Church   88

The Church at New Haven on the Green, Connecticut   90

The Meeting-house at Farmington, Connecticut   91

The Old Ship Church at Hingham, Massachusetts   92

Two Steeples, The Old North and The Old South at Boston   94

Eagle Hall at Milford, the Ancient Meeting-house   97

The Town-house at Hampstead   98

The Meeting-house in the Parish of East Derry   102

A Composite of the Steeples by Sir Christopher Wren   107

The Meeting-house at Ashby, Massachusetts   110

The Meeting-house at Templeton, Massachusetts   111

The Town-house at Fitzwilliam   112

The Portico at Fitzwilliam   114

A Paul Revere Bell at Hancock   123

The Town-house at Jaffrey   124

The Attic at Jaffrey   126

View of Mount Monadnock from the Belfry   128

The Doorway at Hancock with Crucifixion Doors   130

The Church and Town-house at Hancock   132

The Porch at Hancock   134

Two Steeples; Hampstead and Acworth   136

The Meeting-house at Acworth   139

Detail of the Cornice at Acworth   140

The Revere Bell at Acworth   142

The Church and Town-house at Rindge   144

The Meeting-house at Park Hill, Westmoreland   148

The Porch at Park Hill   150

Detail of Front Cornice, Park Hill   152

Detail of Cornice in Doorway, Park Hill   154

The Village Common at Lyme   156

St. John's at Portsmouth   158

The Interior at Union Church, Episcopal Chancel   161

The Union Church at West Claremont   162

The View of Mount Ascutney from the Belfry   163

The Frame in the Attic at West Claremont   164

The Church-yard at Cornish, Trinity Chapel   166

Trinity Episcopal Town-house at Holderness   170

The Interior at Trinity in Holderness   172

The Quaker Meeting-house at Dover   174

The Quaker Meeting-house in Unity, near Acworth   176

The Chapel at Isles of Shoals   178

The First Catholic Chapel at West Claremont   179

The Shaker Meeting-house at Canterbury   180

A Puritan Steeple at Washington, Connecticut   182

The Meeting-house at Brooklyn, Connecticut   183

The East Doorway at Farmington, Connecticut   184

The Meeting-house at Wethersfield, Connecticut   185

The Front of the Colonial Pulpit at Wethersfield   186

Georgian Architecture at Avon, Connecticut   187

The Greek Revival at Windsor, Connecticut   188

The Church on the Green at Springfield, Massachusetts   189

Rocky Hill Meeting-house at Salisbury, Massachusetts   190

The Base of the Tulip Pulpit at Rocky Hill   192

The Choir Stall at Rocky Hill   193

The Base of the Tulip Pulpit at Plymouth, New Hampshire   194

The Pulpit at Rocky Hill   195

The Meeting-house at Sheffield, Massachusetts   196

A Page from Asher Benjamin's Pattern Book   198

The Meeting-house at Rockingham, Vermont   199

The South Doorway at Rockingham   200

The Pulpit at Alna, Maine   202

The Pulpit at Walpole, Maine   205

The German Meeting-house at Waldoboro, Maine   206

The Bulfinch Church at Lancaster, Massachusetts   209

The Bulfinch Influence at Newbury, New Hampshire   210

The Pulpit at Lancaster, Massachusetts   212

The Pulpit at Newbury, New Hampshire   213

The Meeting-house at Webster   214

A Bulfinch Influence at Corser Hill, Webster   216

View of Mount Kearsarge from the Belfry   217

The Vestibule at Corser Hill, Webster   218

The Town Church at Wentworth   220

The Bulfinch Church at Peterborough   222

Flemish Bond and Foot Scrapers at Peterborough   223

The Wine-glass Pulpit at Peterborough   224

The Congregational Church at Newport   226

The Congregational Church at Dover   228

The Greek Revival at Nashua   230

COLONIAL MEETING-HOUSES
IN NEW HAMPSHIRE

Oldest Meeting-house at Newington	1712
Oldest Town-house at Hampstead	1745
The Town-house at North Danville	1760
Quaker Meeting-house at Dover	1760
Park Hill at Westmoreland	1762
The Parish at East Derry	1769
The Town-house at Sandown	1770
The Congregational Church at Amherst	1770
Union Episcopal at West Claremont	1770
Smith Corner Meeting-house at Gilmanton	1774
The Town-house at Jaffrey	1774
The Congregational Church at Wakefield	1785
The Town-house at Henniker	1787
The Town-house at Webster	1789
The Congregational Church at Hopkinton	1789
The Town-house at Washington	1789
The Town-house at New Hampton	1789
The Congregational Church at Salisbury	1790
The Shaker Meeting-house at Canterbury	1792
The Town-house at Canaan Street	1793
The Town-house at Lempster	1795
The Church at North Sutton	1795
The Meeting-house at Barnstead Parade	1796
The Church and Town-house at Rindge	1797

Trinity Episcopal at Cornish Street 1797

Trinity Episcopal at Holderness 1797

The Congregational Church at Exeter 1798

The Congregational Church at Hebron 1800

The Town-house at Fremont 1800

The Chapel at Gossport, Isles of Shoals 1800

Dana Hill Baptist Church 1803

The Town-house at Bridgewater Hill 1804

The Congregational Church at Lyme 1810

The Meeting-house at Allenstown 1815

The Town-house at Fitzwilliam 1817

First Catholic Church at West Claremont 1820

The Quaker Meeting-house at Unity 1820

The Church and Town-house at Hancock 1820

The Congregational Church at Acworth 1821

The Church at Newbury 1821

Corser Hill Church at Webster 1823

First Congregational Church at Dover 1825

First Congregational Church at Keene 1825

The Church at Stoddard 1825

The Town Church at Wentworth 1825

Unitarian Church at Peterborough 1827

The Unitarian Church at Nashua 1827

The Congregational Church at Newport 1828

The Congregational Church at Newcastle 1836

Many church buildings by several denominations 1825

The Second Meeting-house in Concord
Erected 1751 — Burned 1870

CHAPTER I

THE TOWN MEETING-HOUSE

The colonial meeting-houses of New Hampshire prove the quotation, "Architecture is crystallized history." As chemical elements crystallize into symmetrical gems by the process of physical laws so in these aged buildings the spiritual fundamentals of the forefathers: courage, endurance and hope—have solidified into a tangible record beyond rubies in value.

This name, meeting-house, originated in England to designate the place where dissenters from the Church of England were accustomed to assemble for religious worship. Dissenters were forbidden by law to erect a steeple or ring a bell.

A clear differentiation should be noted in the terms church and meeting-house. In the vocabulary of the early settlers in New England, a church was an organization of people, not a building. Not until denominations began to erect their own houses of worship did the name of church apply to the building in New Hampshire after the "Toleration Act" was passed by the legislature in 1819 which permitted the taxpayer to contribute his minister's tax to whatever sect he desired rather than to the "Standing Order," the colloquial expression for the orthodox creed.

In a dual significance—architectural and historical—meeting-houses are entitled to be regarded as colonial. Architecturally, they are distinguished as "New England Colonial," a design unique to this section of the country; "Found in New England and nowhere else" to quote an eminent authority; the product of the artistic skill of obscure, native craftsmen.

Historically, these edifices are noteworthy since no other public buildings existed during the first two centuries of the history of towns. Although the generations that erected them were lacking in wealth and aesthetic surroundings, yet the same innate desire for stately houses of

1

worship animated the families of the Granite State as that which guided their ancestors to construct Canterbury or Durham cathedrals under whose shadows the settlers' grandparents may have played in their childhood in old England.

Abandoned by the trend of population, their very isolation has been the security of a score of those houses now standing. Veneration should kindle when their inestimable worth is appraised. Once destroyed no power can replace them. The primeval forest that supplied the giant oaks for their massive framework and the old growth pines that furnished the boards, approximately a yard in width, for their paneled wainscoting, have vanished forever. With proper precaution, several of these structures on the hill-tops should be bequeathed to many generations as specimens of the genius of the craftsmen of early New England.

The beginnings of New England were sheltered by a trilogy:— dwelling-house, meeting-house and later, school-house, three terse titles that required no elaboration. Although the meeting-house was dedicated to the "Publick worship of God" it was utilized for every public assembly that was considered proper for people to attend. Dancing and gaming, two forbidden pleasures to Puritans, were enjoyed at the taverns or "houses of entertainment." Every deed or word that was permitted in the meeting-house was supervised by the selectmen and the minister even to the approval of "the pieces" which the school children of Rindge were to recite at their annual exhibition.

The importance of the meeting-house in the development of the infant townships cannot be over-estimated. Here was the only building where the entire population could be accommodated; here was the seat of government, both sacred and secular, where the laws of God were taught on Sunday and the laws of men were framed at monthly or, if necessity demanded, at weekly town meetings. Within these walls the taxes were levied, schools established, highways and bridges planned, and the general welfare promoted. Thomas Jefferson said, "Such towns were the wisest invention ever devised by the wit of man for the perfect exercise of self government and for its preservation." The forum of free speech was the New England meeting-house.

Built by taxation from all the voters, the meeting-house was town property. The minister was employed by the town, he was one of its magistrates, his salary was a separate tax on all voters. To estimate the power of the ministers, the lengthy terms of their pastorates should be noted. A half-century was not an exceptional period to serve in one township. Often, the clergyman was the only college bred individual in the earlier settlements, a product of Harvard or Yale, and usually elected to his sacred office immediately after graduation. Although untried and inexperienced, these men grew in wisdom and stature, as did the towns, with the passing of the years.

THE MINISTER'S LOT

When the town was "laid out," one lot was designated as the minister's, sixty or more acres in extent, from which the reverend gentleman was expected to cultivate sustenance for his family. In addition, the minister taught the children of the village to read with the Bible as text book; drew wills for the dying; wrote letters for his parishioners to relatives; officiated at weddings and funerals; and was one of the few persons to "leave town" when called to participate in ordination or dedication ceremonies in other parishes. His chief duty was to prepare two sermons every week strong in their doctrinal import, each not less than two hours in length, which were delivered on the Sabbath with all the eloquence that his personality prompted. In recompense for all these services, a salary of twenty pounds of "lawful money" was considered a generous stipend.

MEETING-HOUSE HILL

With few exceptions the earliest meeting-houses are set upon hill-top sites. Naturally the explorers sought for reasons that prompted their ancestors to select spots which compelled strenuous exertion to approach them. Like the Psalmist the people may have obeyed the admonition to lift up their eyes to the hills from whence came his help since tradition states that, fearing the cloud capped summits as the habitation of the Great Spirit, the Indians shunned the heights thus protecting the meeting-house from their fire brands. A more scientific conclusion is that dry, rocky hill-tops furnished permanent foundations for buildings that were intended to be occupied for several generations, while valleys were often swampy flood-plains before the forests disappeared.

3

COLONIAL MEETING-HOUSES IN NEW HAMPSHIRE

Since the dawn of religious history, summits have been consecrated by holy veneration;—a Fujiyama, a Mount Zion or a Mars Hill. There devotees lavished their creative genius upon temples dedicated to their gods. Scattered among the mountains of Europe are shrines erected to perpetuate vows which were believed to have dispelled pestilence or disaster from the inhabitants in the valleys. At the MacDowell Colony in Peterborough, the Alexander Studio is a reproduction of such a shrine, a votive chapel built six centuries ago by the inhabitants of Saas Pe, a village high in the Alps, to express gratitude to God when He was believed to have stayed a deadly pestilence in answer to the prayers of the people. To this aged chapel Edward MacDowell was wont to ascend for undisturbed meditation when he felt the necessity for divine inspiration to awaken the immortal melodies lying dormant in his soul.

The Alexander Studio
MacDowell Colony
Peterborough

4

THE TOWN MEETING-HOUSE

Likewise, in New Hampshire, a score of hill-tops are hallowed by sanctuaries as venerable as any across the sea where pilgrims who seek for divine guidance may find inspiration for religious motives or artistic dreams. Crowning these heights over a period of two centuries and more colonial meeting-houses have pointed their spires heavenward over the tree-tops with a silent summons to the worship of the God of our fathers; their lofty pulpits have echoed a message of everlasting hope; and through their multipaned windows the glow of golden sunsets has reflected the glory of their hoary past. Let the seeker for truth climb to the crucifixion doors of these white sentinels guarding the graves of the town fathers, let him sit calmly in one of their ancient square pews in the shadow of the high pulpit and over his spirit will steal a sense of abiding peace, a faith in mankind, and an assurance of eternal goodness. As if surrounded by a cloud of celestial witnesses he may seem to hear the Angel of the Lord exclaim, "Put off thy shoes from off thy feet for the place whereon thou standest is holy ground."

Ancient Cemetery
East Derry

5

The Hill-top at Sandown

CHAPTER II

THE MEETING-HOUSE AT SANDOWN

On a breezy November morning, 1932, the explorers definitely instituted their project by a trip to Sandown because here is the only meeting-house in New Hampshire that is preserved as originally designed. Repeatedly the question is hesitatingly asked, "Just where is Sandown?" To orient the reader the following historical facts may be timely.

In 1694, an extensive tract of wilderness, west of Exeter, was granted to a group of proprietors and named King's-town. Many years later this territory was divided into several townships, among them Sandown which was incorporated in 1756. Once upon a time its population numbered over six hundred inhabitants but today about one third of that number till its rugged acres. Two small meeting-houses were successively built before the present structure was completed in 1774.

After stopping to photograph many colonial landmarks:—a Georgian homestead, an ancient town pound, and a charcoal kiln—the travelers realized that mid-day was approaching before we left Chester on route 102. Accordingly, a sunny spot, sheltered from the chilling wind by a background of pines, was selected for the noon picnic. Our drive of one hundred miles caused full justice to be given to the lunch basket's contents. Fortified for a long afternoon of study we were soon on our way and, before many miles had been covered, we rounded a curve and the view of Sandown greeted us from the top of a steep hill. Immediately the photographer alighted to slowly climb the height, gathering pictures along the way, while the others drove on to interview Mr. Thomas R. Shaw, the custodian, who graciously accompanied us and answered our numerous questions throughout the afternoon.

Meager town records are the only source of information; no definite accounts are in existence that describe the construction of the edifice. In the house occupied by Mr. Shaw a short distance from the meeting-

7

The Town Pound

As was usual in early townships, the high stone walls
of the town pound stand across the narrow highway from
the meeting-house. Here straying domestic animals were
confined until claimed by their owner and the price of their
fodder paid to the town pound-keeper.

house, lived a carpenter, Peter Colby, who may have been the master-builder as examples of his workmanship indicate the hand of a craftsman and his tools are in the possession of Mr. Shaw. Untarnished by time remain the distinguishing evidences that skilled workmen planned in Sandown as the illustrations manifest far better than words can describe them.

Regardless of the discomfort of that cold November wind, our attention was first given to the exterior. Many distinctive marks dated this building. Narrow, "feathered" clapboards, relics of an eighteenth century custom of tapering the ends and overlapping them an inch or more, are fastened by hand-wrought nails; many panes in the windows show the blemishes of old blown glass, and the three doorways, each different in design from the others, deserve careful observation. Finally the dimensions were measured:—length, fifty-four feet and breadth, forty-eight.

The Rear Window

The semicircular frame of the pulpit window is composed of several curved mouldings.

The South Doorway

THE SOUTH DOORWAY

This frame required a year of handicraft. Its distinctive colonial marks are: grooved pilasters; delicate mouldings; Latin crosses between the panels giving the names of Crucifixion Doors and also Witch Doors because no evil spirit was supposed to pass the cross. Feathered joints may be seen in the narrow clapboards near the left window.

The Goblet Pulpit

THE GOBLET PULPIT

This consisted of the deacons' pew, the stairway to the pulpit, the sacred desk, the pulpit window, and the sounding board.

The Staircase of the Goblet Pulpit

THE STAIRCASE VIEW

Here may be noted the hand-turned spindles of the balustrade; the goblet projection of the pulpit; the drop-leaf shelf on the deacons' pew used for the plate at communion, and the gavel at town meetings; the number plate on the door of the wall pew; the wide panels of the balcony parapet; the "free pew" above it.

The Sacred Desk

The seat for the clergy was narrow; the
cushions around the rail were well padded; and
the height of the minister was accommodated by
two removable four inch planks.

THE MEETING-HOUSE AT SANDOWN

Then the south door was approached. No deacons were waiting to conduct the visitors to the front seats of honor, as was the custom in 1774. That ceremony could not be repeated when the minister, the Reverend Josiah Cotton, was welcomed by the deacons and, as he bowed and smiled to the right and left, was escorted down the center aisle to ascend the pulpit stairs while the deacons entered the door of their pew at the right of the stairway. However, we hastened down the aisle to stand spellbound before the colonial pulpit. What a revelation of craftmanship! Its pine surface had been stained a walnut brown. Weathered by the lights and shadows of one hundred and sixty summers and winters, it gleamed in the afternoon sunshine although its finish is unlike the polish of hand rubbed furniture. The graceful curves of the mouldings carved from blocks of pine, the fluted pilasters and grooved panels, held in place by wooden pegs, excited our admiration. Most striking was the huge canopy or "sounding board" suspended without visible support from the north wall. No wonder little children watched during the long Sunday sermons with fear that this bell-like structure would fall upon the minister's head, for thirty feet above the floor the elongated knob just escaped the ceiling. Mr. Shaw contributed the information that but three pulpits of like design were known to have been erected, called the "Goblet" pattern because the base of the projection of the pulpit itself was delicately curved like the bowl of a silver goblet and the tapering lines to the deacons' pew resembled the slender stem of the wine cups for the sacrament.

The afternoon sunbeams illuminated the room which otherwise might have impressed us as severely plain with its bare, whitewashed walls divided into sections by the rude posts of the frame that projected from the plaster and displayed the rough marks left by the blade of the broad-ax that squared them from tough white oak logs. However, the sparkle of the thirty-two small panes in each window served as ornaments around the rough walls and the sunbeams reflected in the walnut-brown panels of the balcony parapet and stall pews provided a cheerful glow of warmth. After staying several hours on that November day in this most comfortable atmosphere, we realized that even on a cold winter Sunday if the sun shone and the room was filled with people, the temperature would not be unbearably frigid especially for those who were furnished with hot coals in their soapstone foot warmers.

The Front Seat of Honor

Finally we were glad to rest on the narrow board seat of an ancient square pew, meditating upon past centuries until the very walls seemed to speak. Imagination pictured that old custom of brides and grooms stealing to the pews that were conspicuously placed in the balcony on either side of the pulpit, in the midst of a Sabbath hour of worship. There the couple clasped hands and pirouetted around and around to display their wedding finery while the minister continued his discourse apparently unmindful that the attention of his audience was distracted from the thirteenth point of his afternoon sermon.

As we stood, the hinged board seat lifted and fell with a resounding clatter upon the wooden supports awakening our sympathy for the youngsters who claimed the privilege of dropping those seats with a bang after standing, as was the custom, sometimes more than an hour during the "long prayer."

Ascending the balcony stairs, ornamented with spindles like the balustrade of the pulpit, we understood why the elders paid an extra

18

THE MEETING-HOUSE AT SANDOWN

The Front Balcony

number of pounds to purchase the balcony pews placed two steps above the floor, around the walls. Here restless children could be amused or an afternoon nap indulged without seeming to be too conspicuous for the high sides were ornamented by still higher frames and spindles, the latter now stolen by vandals who visited the building during the gay nineties. It is reported that this house was a favorite rendezvous among students from the academy at Exeter and that at one visit they so despoiled the interior that the authorities of Sandown caused a heavy fine to be exacted from the marauders.

Within the front parapet opposite the pulpit are mortises where the wall of the choir stall once was attached, but in 1860 an organ took the place of the bass viol and several pews were removed to accommodate a modern choir. Also in 1835 stoves were installed, the pipe passing through the ceiling to a small chimney in the attic. What quantities of fuel must have been consumed to preceptibly moderate the atmosphere of that high posted room!

19

The Frame in the Attic

This eighteenth century frame in the attic
has four tie-beams with struts to the double rafters which are wedged with small blocks, called "the
locked joint." Double rafters were usually found
before 1800. Note the marks left by the adz on
the foot-square oak timbers.

THE MEETING-HOUSE AT SANDOWN

Fortunately Mr. Shaw has provided stairs to the attic because here is the most intriguing section of the meeting house. The measuring tape was busily applied to oak beams that had been cut from giant tree trunks as tall as the length of the building and equivalent in diameter to produce timbers a foot square. Wavy marks on the smaller struts were left by saws but all the plates, tie-beams and trusses were adzed.

One unusual but convenient addition was the "locked joints" which can be discerned in the illustrations. Small wedges of wood were driven into the mortises which could be knocked out to release the pins more easily if the frame should be taken apart as so often happened.

A tradition of the raising is called a strike among the workmen. Several days were required to fasten all the timbers in place and plenty of rum was supposed to be furnished. Late in the afternoon the rum barrel was found to be empty and warning was given that unless the supply was replenished, no work would be done on the morrow. The nearest port where the barrel could be filled was miles distant at Newburyport. Unwilling that the work should be delayed, the master-builder is said to have driven his team to this seaport and returned the same night with drafts of rum for the workmen. Considering the rough trails of that period the story, if true, illustrates a persistence of the New England character.

Another tale has been attributed to a janitor of a generation ago. One Sabbath in the midst of his sermon, the minister accidently pushed the Bible over the side of the tall pulpit into the deacons' pews below. Aghast at the consequence of this startling mistake the agitated clergyman leaned over the pulpit and cried, "Deacon, deacon, are you hurt?" Assured that no damage had been inflicted to the heads of the dignified officials, the service was resumed.

As the sun sank towards the horizon, gratitude was expressed to Mr. Shaw for his courtesy and the trail of the pioneers was followed to Kingston. There a call was enjoyed at the homestead of the Signer of the Declaration of Independence, Dr. Josiah Bartlett, where the present Mrs. Bartlett displayed her heirlooms to her guests. Then on to Exeter to dine before the long drive to Plymouth.

Clouds settled over the heavens, darkness covered the landscape. Tired but satisfied by the events of the day we retraced the miles to our homes where we arrived just before mid-night.

21

CHAPTER III

BUILDING A MEETING-HOUSE

In the charters for townships granted to corporations of proprietors, a stipulation was usually included that a meeting-house should be built at the expense of the corporation. Small log houses, approximately twenty feet square, fulfilled this obligation. At Barnstead where the charter called for a meeting-house within four years of the date of the grant, even before a settler had purchased a tract in that part of the wilderness, workmen were sent from Newington to erect a log cabin for the worship of God. Rev. Joseph Adams, mentioned elsewhere in connection with Newington, was one of the proprietors. "Believing that some cere-

The Log Meeting-house at Penny Cook,
now Concord, 1726

mony was proper," a tradition exists that "a workman entered the finished house and uttered a prayer, the only religious service ever to occur within its walls."

The evolution of the meeting-house developed in successive stages from log cabins to the ornate structures with steeples and porticoes of the Connecticut Valley. As soon as a sufficient number of settlers had become well established and able to pay the necessary taxes, a framed building superseded the log cabin; then, after a half-century, if increased population demanded and financial prosperity permitted, a third meeting-house would be erected adequate in size and suitable to the architectural standards of the township.

Let no one delude himself into believing that the "gude auld days" were less disposed to factional disputes or political quarrels than is the twentieth century. If the early records of town meetings are reliable sources, certainly they represent the forefathers as expressing their convictions in the presence of all the voters with a bluntness of speech which ignored both courtesy and Puritan sanctimoniousness. Rather explicit personalities were employed in arguments that were often supplemented with oaths and occasionally pursued to fisticuffs between opposing factions. Which section of the town should be honored with a building, the amount of taxation to be levied, and the membership of the building committee were fruitful sources for endless disputes. In several towns—Hopkinton, Raymond, or Canterbury for example—a committee from neighboring towns was summoned to whose judgment the selection of a site was delegated since no agreement could be arranged in the town meeting.

AMHERST, A TYPICAL EXAMPLE

Amherst is an excellent example of the evolution of successive meeting-houses. After King Philip's War, the General Court of Massachusetts decided to compensate its victorious soldiers with tracts of land in Maine and New Hampshire, all this territory being then under the jurisdiction of the Bay Colony.

Accordingly in 1685 Souhegan West, now Amherst, was granted but nothing came of this first charter. Again in 1727 a new charter was drawn and six years later the grantees met on "ye common in Boston

The Congregational Church at Amherst
Built 1770 — Remodeled 1836

BUILDING A MEETING-HOUSE

to lay out ye territory." In 1734 the proprietors of Souhegan West again met at Salem, Massachusetts where many of them lived, and soon a committee was appointed to "lay out a place whereon to erect the public meeting-house for the worship of God, public burying place, training field, and three home lots of sixty acres each: one for the first settled minister, one for the ministry—meaning the Church of England—and one for the schools." By 1741 fourteen families were settled in the grant and in 1760 the town was incorporated under the name of Amherst in honor of General Jeffrey Amherst, Commander of the British Forces in America. The town fathers planned wisely. No village in New Hampshire is landscaped with greater beauty. The training field is surrounded by wide, elm shaded streets, each lined by stately colonial homes.

After the boundary dispute between the Bay Colony and New Hampshire was decided in 1740, Amherst was included within the latter colony. Governor Benning Wentworth granted a charter to a small town adjoining, called Munson which is now absorbed into surrounding townships. No meeting-house was erected in Munson; its settlers chose to worship in Amherst thus "getting their preaching free" for no minister's tax could be levied upon Munsonites although they crowded their neighbor's meeting-house beyond its capacity.

The necessity for a larger assembly room was apparent yet the proposition was voted down in successive town meetings by those individualists who objected to paying taxes for the religious accommodation of Munson. Finally on October fourth, 1770 the town voted to build a new meeting-house on the training field, dimensions to be seventy-five feet by forty-five, a generous size, and to raise one hundred fifty pounds of lawful money to defray the initial expenses. Lawful money —Spanish coins in many places—was not easily obtained in those days when the colonies did not possess sufficient wealth to permit coinage. Another town meeting in that same month voted to cut the size to seventy by forty feet but to build a steeple on the west gable and a porch over the east doorway. Some objections were offered to the training field as the site; also, antagonism was aroused when the committee to build was appointed. So, one trusted citizen refused to serve to the consternation of the voters but, at length, Deacon Barker accepted the responsibility of chairman of the building committee.

25

FRAMING THE MEETING-HOUSE

Deacon Barker and his assistants were expected to cruise through the forests for five straight oaks whose trunks could supply timbers seventy feet in length for the sills and the plates for the north and south walls and ridge-pole of the frame. Not less than fifty other logs, forty to fifty feet in length and eighteen inches in diameter, must be cut for the sleepers to support the floor and for the tie-beams for the ceiling and for the posts for the walls. In addition, several hundred beams of varying sizes must be prepared for braces and roof timbers; a gigantic task when only man power and oxen could be relied upon. Recall that expression, "Snaking out a log" as you picture the tortuous path every one must travel from the forest to the training field, there to be squared with an adz to the required dimensions. Then housewrights cut mortises in the ends of certain beams and tenons on others and bored holes for the graduated wooden pins to wedge the joints together. Finally all the sills, plates and posts were laid in place on the ground and firmly pinned, wall by wall; all the braces were planned and the trusses for the roof pinned in order. Then the frame was ready to raise. Scores of wide planks were sawn either by pit saws by man power or in clumsy saw mills with up and down saws of that period, for covering for the walls and roof.

The stability of the meeting-house depended upon the ability and experience of the master-carpenter. The earlier buildings were often faulty in structural quality. Experience had not taught the necessity of exact measurements, of closely fitted mortise and tenon joints, and of allowance for the changes caused by drying the green timbers. A frame that could support the weight of the ceiling and roof without interior posts required mechanical methods that only the expert housewrights appreciated. Timbers must have sufficient diameter to permit long tenons and deep mortises; struts were skillfully braced from posts to tie-beams and to the trusses of the roof. In fact, like a bridge, the building seemed to hang from the framework of its roof. In those edifices that have stood over a century and a half the engineering of the frame is the secret of their stability through all the years.

26

BUILDING A MEETING-HOUSE

No two frames, of those that were photographed, were constructed by exactly the same pattern but all followed the same general principles that had been understood for many centuries in Europe. White oak was the usual material with some old growth pine included in the later meeting-houses. Cellars were unknown, foundations were the common field stone of the hill-side. Quarried bases did not appear until well into the nineteenth century.

In a brief time for such an undertaking this task was so far accomplished that a town meeting was called on August twenty-sixth, 1771 that voted "the building committee provide drink for raising the frame of the meeting-house not exceeding eight barrels for such as shall do the labor of raising and for all spectators" and "one barrel of brown sugar for use of laborers and spectators to be distributed according to the discretion of said committee." Amherst was generous in its entertainment since two barrels of rum was the average supply that was purchased in most of the towns.

THE RAISING

A raising was a gala event. The Herculean task demanded all the muscular strength of the countryside. The fathers believed that their energy must be stimulated with plenty of New England rum. Certainly every man must exert his utmost power if accidents were to be avoided. The green timbers were ponderous since white oak weighs when dry forty-eight pounds to the cubic foot and from one fifth to one half more when green, the probable average was sixty-five pounds per cubic foot of the entire frame. A single truss for the roof weighed nearly ten thousand pounds. Buildings the size of Amherst's meeting-house required four trusses and two gable ends to support the roof, and the ridge pole would weigh approximately five thousand pounds. After the walls' frames stood entirely fixed upon their granite foundations and firmly pinned at all the joints, doubtless the trusses for the roof were elevated with tackle and screw jacks with men for the motive power. Poles with iron spikes in the ends were used as levers to gradually push the massive frames of the walls upright with constant danger that one man might fail to do his part at a critical moment. The carpenter in charge of the work was supposed to risk his life by riding up on the

The King Post Trusses

Here are the timbers that support the roof, two king posts and the girth between them set lengthwise of the frame with the pins to fasten the cross beams. Here braces extend from the post to the tie-beams and to the double rafters, on either side.

gallery girth to supervise the pinning of the joints at the four corners as the several frames were raised. Usually the west wall was raised first, and held upright with poles and ropes until another could be fastened to it. No wonder that housewives filled their brick ovens with beans and corn bread, pies and pound cake, for a noonday feast was a necessary part of the festivities.

No contest of the present can surpass the excitement of a raising with all the customs that developed around this event. Every man exhibited his muscular power and fame was established for the skilled workman. Heavy timbers were lifed single handed and other feats of strength displayed. Youths clambered in a wild race to be first to straddle the ridge pole the prize being the right to "wet down the pole" with a bottle of rum and to give a name to the building. The most level headed man in town climbed to the ridge to drive the pegs that fixed the trusses to the pole. Sad to relate accidents were frequent episodes as heads were confused by the effect of the beverages. At one raising in New Hampshire the minister's son, a brilliant student at Dartmouth, fell to his death while racing to the upper timbers. Writing about the events of the day in Portsmouth when the South Meeting-house was raised, the minister expressed "gratitude to God that no fatal accident marred the day." In Plymouth when the women spectators pleaded that a steeple might be erected, Colonel David Webster, first townsman, is said to have stood on his head on the ridgepole and stretched his six feet of length into the air as he shouted, "I will be your steeple."

To return to Amherst's raising, which was, indeed, a famous event, Sam Wilkins, son of the minister, chief champion of wrestling, ran a short distance with the chairman of the building committee on his shoulders, a feat to be remembered as the load was a "sixth of a ton." Several weeks were required to finish the skeleton framework. Amherst held another town meeting which voted that the building committee "were authorized to procure a sufficiency of victuals and drink for such as such labor in raising said house while laboring, viz., one, two or three meals a day, as laborers should require."

Delays were expected; again taxes must be assessed to provide funds to purchase clapboards, shingles, and "glazing" as the glass panes were called. So long did a neighboring town of Bedford postpone the use of its panes, doubtless ordered from England, that they were rented to several householders "to be used until such a time as the town should need them."

THE AUCTION

Finally when the walls, floor, gallery and roof were completed, all was in readiness for the interior furnishings. Another feast day was proclaimed for the vendue, an auction of the floor space for the pews. In some of the towns heads of families purchased whatever number of square feet were required to build a pew that would accommodate the number of persons in their family, paying higher prices for the wall pews in the balcony than for the ground floor. This method provided the amount necessary to erect the pulpit, the paneled parapet for the balcony, and the walls and seats of the pews. Amherst voted on November fourteenth, 1772, "to sell the pew ground on the lower floor of the meeting-house to the highest bidder, money to defray the expenses of finishing the house." Thus can be estimated that a year and three months elapsed between the date of the raising and the auction.

The carpenters had completed their part of the work; now the interior finishers, or joiners—as they were called—and woodcarvers consumed two more years to finish the building. Their task was accomplished by manual labor supplemented by tools that were crude, indeed, in contrast to the mechanisms of today. The wide boards for the parapet and walls of pews were cut from logs by skilled sawyers with pit saws. To saw a plank thirty inches wide with a uniform thickness of an inch and a half was no simple achievement. The log was rolled over a hole in the ground. One man stood on the log and pushed a saw down through the wood to another workman beneath in the pit who pushed the saw back, repeatedly, until the plank was severed.

Woodcarvers manipulated a set of thirty or more small hand-planes. Each tool was fitted with a sharp knife whose blade was so adjusted, either straight or curved, that it carved a moulding or gouged the flutes of a pillar. Clumsy hand-lathes, turned by a crank or a treadle, manufactured the hundreds of spindles for balustrades or "banisters" for the pews' walls. Every piece for a corbel that was attached to the eaves or the frieze of a parapet, every dentil in a pediment for doorways, every classic capital above a pillar or pilaster was carved by the patient toil of a craftsman's expert hands. No steam or electrical power was available; the force was human energy.

It seems impossible today to gauge the necessary number of hours or the size of various groups of skilled laborers that were required. Wages were exceedingly low in comparison with even unskilled labor today. A building of the size at Amherst was erected for six or seven thousand dollars.

Paint was expensive and seldom applied to the exterior before 1800 but stains of domestic manufacture colored the pine paneled interior. The hardware was fashioned by the village blacksmith by his own designs. Not nails but wooden pegs fastened the many and various sections of the furniture together. An examination of a high pulpit illustrates the expertness of a joiner's art. The pegs are inconspicuous.

Only hours of minute scrutiny of both the exterior and the interior embellishments of the colonial meeting-houses will reveal to the consciousness that creative art was achieved with native white pine in New England equivalent to that in marble in Europe.

If the picture of the meeting-house in Brooklyn, Connecticut is noted, the appearance of Amherst's completed building may be imagined, before alterations were made in 1835.

THE DEDICATION

When the building was completed, the day for the dedication was appointed, a time of solemn ceremony which was attended not only by the entire population but by clergymen from a wide radius who were invited to participate in the program. January nineteenth, 1774—three years and fifteen days from the beginning of the structure—was the appointed day in Amherst. Without heat in this large new house of worship, the courage of the people astonishes modern minds; mid-winter would impress the church of today as unsuitable for lengthy ceremonies. However, Parson Wilkins preached a sermon "Thought to have been historical, of matters pertaining to the settlement of the town" although no record remains of his discourse. Visiting clergymen were entertained at dinner by Parson Wilkins with the principal dish, "hasty pudding and milk"—a contrast to the "eight barrels" for the raising.

Changes were sure to appear as years passed. On March fourth, 1774, the town voted against purchasing a bell also not to allow singers seats "that Psalmody may be carried on with greater regulation." Experience changed the mind of the citizens evidently because four years later a vote passed that "the seats in the front gallery be granted for the use of a number of persons skilled in singing." Again in 1796 the consent of the parish was sought that the bass viol might be used in the meeting-house on Sundays "to assist the singers at the time of public worship." Again the approval of the voters was not obtained. In 1818 a meeting of citizens was called to consider the "expediency of establishing Sunday Schools in town;" in the same year in March the town refused to purchase stoves. Not daunted, the advocates for warmth circulated a subscription paper which provided funds to install stoves six years later, no objections being offered by the voters to this financial arrangement.

The following story which is copied as it was told in Dunbarton, illustrates the opposition of many people to the introduction of stoves which were considered a dangerous invention.

"Time was when the people thought they must be more modern and have some heat in the church. A few fought it and said if the Grace of God was not enough to keep them warm, they had better stay at home. Two old maids fought bitterly, but the majority won, and the stove was ordered from Boston, and was set up, but the pipe was too short and so they did not 'fire up' the first Sunday, but put it up temporarily, so they could see how it was going to look. The 'two unconfisticated blessings' came with their fans and sat through the service fanning all the time. 'Holy Poker' but they were mad when they found there was no fire." (as told)

Another tale from a later period in Hillsborough is amusing.

"The only method of heating the meeting-house in the early days was the foot stove.

"Some time after the new church was built a furnace was installed which met the disfavor of some, particularly in the case of one old lady, Mary Ann by name.

"The first time she came down the aisle, she stopped when she came to the register in the middle of the aisle, lifted her skirts ankle high, jumped across, thence passing down to her seat in the front row as though nothing unusual had happened. The good old lady was not taking any chances in keeping warm by such 'new-fangle, cast iron contraption as that,' she said.

"On seating herself she proceeded to light her little foot stove paying no attention to the titter from the boys and some of the grown-ups in the gallery.

"There have been some Sundays since that time when we should have liked to 'cuddle up' to that little foot stove ourselves."

In the following year, 1819, the Toleration Act passed the General Court which separted church and state. Within a few years many towns were thankful to release their property to a church organization. Accordingly, Amherst voted to sell its meeting-house at auction in 1833 though not without reservations. The First Congregational Church and Society were the purchasers after agreeing to allow the town to use the building for all town meetings as long a time as it might wish; the bell, clock, belfry, and tower to remain the property of the town with the right to the Society to pass through the tower doors, ring the bell for funerals and public worship and on other occasions, with a clear statement, "without expense to the town." Owners of pews were to have the right to them and owners of stoves and organ to be allowed to remove their property. The purchasers agreed to keep the house in repair or it should revert to the town. Certainly the voters of Amherst still cherished their meeting-house. During following decades the town maintained these reservations but at length all claims, with the exception of the town clock, were deeded to the Congregational Society.

The building then stood on the training field. The Society purchased the lot on the opposite side of the street in 1836 and moved the building there. The east porch was removed; the west porch broadened to permit stairways to the balconies; and the foundations elevated to accommodate a chapel in the basement. The steeple remains as when built in 1772, the oldest now in New Hampshire.

Such is a typical history of a meeting-house. The thirty and more now standing could duplicate, in general conditions, the same problems and experiences. With self-sacrifice to finance them and with pride in their ownership, the forefathers established standards of religion and of government in these buildings that have been the foundation of the civilization of all New England. *18800*

The Meeting-house at North Danville
1760

CHAPTER IV

EARLY MEETING-HOUSES

Although Sandown has been illustrated as the most complete speci-men of early meeting-house architecture which is preserved in New Hampshire at the present time, several other structures deserve recogni-tion, not only for their individual history but also for their particular contribution to our knowledge of decided variations in architectural de-velopment in the different towns.

NORTH DANVILLE

In the northern section of old King's-town is a meeting-house that antedates Sandown by fifteen years at North Danville. As early as 1739, long before the menace of Indian raids had become unknown, two families had built their cabins in this wilderness, who were followed within twenty years by a sufficient number of pioneers to permit them to demand a separate township which was incorporated in 1760 with the name of Hawke in honor of the British admiral. Four years later an adjoining township was separated from Exeter and Brentwood called Poplin. To this day may be found along the old range roads several granite boundary posts with a rude letter "H" chisled on one side and a "P" on the opposite side to mark the dividing line that the surveyors designated between these towns.

Immediately, the industrious settlers of Hawke commenced to frame a meeting-house that in the then brief period of three years was ready for town meetings. Only in the frame of the south doorway and the hoods over the front windows were the outside walls embellished; wisely the beautification of the interior received the benefit of the meager taxes. Here is the oldest high pulpit in New Hampshire, displaying craftsman-ship in every line of its panels and fluted pilasters and shapely sounding board. The balcony parapet of old growth pine panels could not be reproduced today. In contrast to this skilled workmanship are the hewn timbers that project their rough surfaces from the plastered walls.

After several generations had worshiped here and enacted the regulations of town affairs, changes in community sentiment, both sacred and secular, naturally divided the inhabitants. With little mental effort the indignation of the citizens can be appreciated when the news circulated one morning that one faction of dissenters had performed an act of vandalism during the previous night, of irreparable consequences. The description of the custodian to the explorers was vivid. "You see, some of them wanted to dance. So, they ripped out the pews on the lower floor one night." Said another proud descendant of those early builders, indignation filling her voice, "They never did dance a step there. The people were so enraged that no one dared to attempt it." Sadly the shattered pine panels were collected into the gallery to await a day when

The Quaint Sounding Board
of the oldest Puritan pulpit in New England

a surplus of taxes might permit this sacrilege to be obliterated. Years passed before an aged woman left a small bequest to her son who returned to his mother's old home in the summer of 1936. Generously he gave the legacy to erase the profanation from the sight of men. On an August Sabbath the citizens celebrated a rededication of their restored meeting-house with true pride in their heritage of more than a century and three quarters of accumulated history.

In 1836, the fame of the British admiral had so diminished that the name of the town was changed to Danville.

THE TOWN HOUSE AT FREMONT

Poplin did not exhibit the same eagerness for a commodious meeting-house as its neighbor, Hawke. Not until 1800 was the present town-house raised. The dimensions were less than the house in Danville but space in the interior was conserved by building a porch over the east and the west doorways in which the stairs ascended to the gallery. Time has not dealt kindly with the furniture. It is reported that when the sounding board fell above the high pulpit, the janitor disregarded its value and cut it into kindling for his fire.

One relic has fortunately been preserved intact—long may it remain —since it is the only specimen of its kind in New Hampshire. This reference is to the choir-stall in the front gallery opposite the pulpit. There is the small platform in the center where the precentor stood with his bass viol, flanked on either side by two rows of benches and a breast-high book rest whose slanted top accommodated the glances of the singers toward those tune books that opened their two feet of length to display those ancient scores in minor key that were considered sufficiently mournful and solemn to be the proper music for orthodox worship. Underneath was a shelf to receive the "Psalmist," that even more ancient collection of paraphrased selections from the songs of David and the other poets in the Bible.

Poplin became Fremont in 1854 in honor of the western hero of that name.

The Choir Stall

THE CHOIR STALL IN FREMONT

This pew was reserved for those who were "skilled in singing." Along the parapet of the east and west balconies were slip pews for the accommodation of persons who did not own square pews. The women occupied the east side and the men the left.

The Meeting-house at Fremont

Porches over the east and the west doorways contained staircases to the galleries.

EARLY MEETING-HOUSES

ALLENSTOWN

First Christian Church

erected 1815

Restored by Buntin Chapter, D. A. R.

1909

Church organized July 10, 1807

Hall Burgin, Clerk

Such is the inscription on a tablet that is fastened to the outside wall of the small meeting-house that is hidden among the pines at Allenstown. On one Sunday in August the shutters are opened and the doors unlocked for worshipers who arrive from far and wide to revisit this spot and renew old friendships.

Once upon a time, more than a century ago, a village grew to some importance with its tavern and its brickyard. Once the burying ground surrounded the meeting-house. A tradition exists that a greedy farmer, owner of a thousand acres, removed the stones that marked each resting-place and used the clearing for a wheat field. Now a pine grove, that murmurs a continuous requiem, is a memorial planted by the Buntin Chapter in remembrance of the founders above their unknown dust.

Clerk Hall Burgin is believed to have written on the door of the meeting-house this peculiar couplet:—

"Little meeting-house without a steeple, God bless the minister, but the devil take the people."

Whatever the motive behind the rhyme, time has erased the memory of its origin.

Interior at Allenstown

No meeting-house in the state "dignified" its pews with such economy of space, not an inch is wasted. Around the walls on high platforms are family pews. At the same height, the pulpit is surrounded by a pine parapet. On either side of the center aisle and facing it rather than the pulpit, are rows of seats, the lower on the level of the floor, the others raised by a series of step-like platforms until the occupants of the rear "slips" are on the same elevation as the floor of the pulpit.

Allenstown was granted in 1722 to the heirs of Samuel Allen, first provincial governor appointed by the king, to compensate them for claims that involved a long contest about a purchase of land from the heirs of John Mason, the first proprietor of New Hampshire Grants in 1623. The township was named for the provincial governor by his heirs. Only the name perpetuates those ancient quarrels; the forest has reclaimed the sandy meadows except for the little meeting-house lot which serves as a memorial to an extinct village on a by-way in central New Hampshire.

COLONIAL MEETING-HOUSES IN NEW HAMPSHIRE

SMITH MEETING-HOUSE IN GILMANTON

Beyond the early townships of the coastal plain, no place in New Hampshire offers more attractions for the antiquarian than Gilmanton. In the dead of winter, 1761, the first family, Benjamin Mudgett and wife, after walking the last twelve miles on snow-shoes, arrived at a log house that had been prepared the previous summer. Other families followed in the spring and within two years a settled minister and school teacher combined was one of the residents. Ten years passed, then in 1774, Rev. Isaac Smith held a service in Jotham Gilman's barn representing "the Standing Order." So numerous were the Baptists in this new settlement that the two sects separated and each maintained its house of worship and paid its minister. Parson Smith is recorded as "a solemn, searching preacher" who received an annual salary of one hundred seventy-five dollars, a generous sum for that time. Immediately, at the top of the hill since known as "Smith's Corner" from the remarkable reputation of this preacher, a small meeting-house was erected which remains in constant use to this day although its interior has been completely modernized.

On the slope of the hill is a cemetery whose ancient headstones mark the graves of many soldiers of the American Revolution and bear the names of families distinguished by honors in state and nation.

Gradually from Gilmanton were carved Guilford, Belmont, a part of Laconia and Weirs whose history is included in the beginnings of this township. From Smith's Corner the population spread into other villages. Gilmanton Center became the intellectual section where lived the wealthy manufacturers of bog iron that was mined in the swamps surrounding the numerous lakes of the township. Beautiful homes of Georgian architecture beside the elm shaded streets are excellent testimonials to their owners' culture. Today may be seen the Congregational church of Bulfinch influence, built in 1828 on the village green and adjacent to the academy which was chartered in 1794 with tuition at a dollar per term. A department of a "Theological Seminary" was added "to aid in providing an adequate supply of able, humble, zealous, and laborious ministers," the first of this branch in the state.

The Smith Corner Meeting-house
1774

DANA HILL MEETING-HOUSE

Another lonely little church on another by-way bears the honored title of a family that contributed its talents to several generations, in New Hampton and Ashland. Dr. Simeon Dana came to New Hampton in 1803, fresh from his college days at Dartmouth, a graduate physician who offered to practice medicine, teach singing school or dancing steps to anyone who desired his services. He soon became associated with the Baptists, accepted their doctrines and was ordained to their ministry. During his life he preached to the souls and doctored the bodies of his townsmen. Riding his faithful horse and carrying his healing balms in his saddle-bags, he received a fee of twenty-five cents for his professional calls but no salary was paid for his sermons since the Freewill Baptists believed that no money should be paid for "divining." The doctor lived at the top of a long, steep hill above the meeting-house, bestowing his name upon the entire neighborhood.

45

The Dana Hill Meeting-house

This building stands as originally constructed in 1803. Although the diminutive size prevented its builders from following the plans of larger structures, yet the three doorways, and many paned windows are here. Also, the front porch over the door of honor is the original design.

EARLY MEETING-HOUSES

In 1800, the Freewill Baptists withdrew their support from the Standing Order of New Hampton and built their little meeting-house. At this period, the Baptists throughout New Hampshire were gaining thousands of followers through the evangelistic preaching of several talented speakers. Before the meeting-house was furnished with more than rude benches, a quarterly meeting assembled at Dana church with an attendance of several hundred persons. Some of these people traveled from the coast on horse-back, bringing their food and covering for out-of-door living while scores joined them along their way. Singing and shouting, they assembled in the famous camp meeting style around Dana church.

Nine years after, three hundred dollars was agreed upon as the price to Stephen S. Magoon to finish the house. Because the posts are too low to permit a gallery, the pews are built upon platforms, the highest near the walls, the several tiers graduated lower and lower until the three slip pews are on the floor below the tall pulpit. "How I used to tremble as a boy as I sat in one of those pews and heard the elders preach about hell and eternal punishment" said a man of the party who accompanied the explorers on their visit to Dana Hill.

The Gordon family of New Hampton has been prominent both in that town and in Boston churches. Guided by their experience, restoration was begun several years ago and today every spindle is in place in the banisters of the pews and all signs of decay have been erased. Summer Sabbaths find children assembling for classes in Bible study and occasional preaching services are held in July and August.

From the Dana farm-house a son, Dr. John Dana, departed to practice his profession in Ashland where his talented daughter was born, known throughout New England as Martha Dana Shepard, an able pianist of a half century ago.

A short distance from Dana Hill, in the very center of New Hampton stands its de-capitated meeting-house of 1789. The upper story was removed when the population sought a new center for village life but the March town meeting always convenes in this old "town-house."

Northward a few miles on the top of Bridgewater Hill may be found another remodeled town-house that once resembled Sandown, where the voters assemble on election days.

CHAPTER V

THE EARLIEST TOWNSHIPS

That the foundations of the first meeting-house in New Hampshire as well as the oldest now in existence should be in that section which was originally colonized would not be disputed. With the intention of viewing these two venerable landmarks, the explorers prepared for an early departure, one April morning, toward the seacoast.

Their initial discovery of that trip was at Rochester where the central square is guarded by a statue of Rev. Amos Main, ordained to minister in the beginning of the township. Across the square, although unseen, timbers that support the walls of the Congregational church were, long ago, a part of the frame of a second edifice on Norway Plains, named from the long-needled pines of this region. Farther south is the birthplace of Rochester on Haven's Hill, its original meeting-house lot distinguished by a bronze tablet placed by Mary Torr Chapter of the Daughters of the American Revolution. What appears as a modern New England farm house across the highway was the parsonage of 1760. Not far distant is a venerable relic, the Dame homestead, said to have been the first framed dwelling between Dover and Canada in 1758 which seemed to demand and received the respect of our door-step call.

DOVER POINT

Following the Province Road through Dover, innumerable interruptions might have detained the party if Hilton's Point had not been the dominant objective. Speeding travelers have no conception of the historical aspect of the peaceful valley. Here are farms that were cleared by pioneers who heard the warwhoop of murderous Indians; here was the outpost of white men until 1725. Like other thousands, we had never stopped to read the legend upon the bronze tablet fastened upon a reinforcing wall of granite so close to the concrete that parking beside the hurrying traffic is foolhardy. That day we stood upon the summit of Dover Point, the spot first dedicated to the worship of God in New Hampshire. Gazing at the converging streams, east to the Bellamy River and west at the Piscataqua, we attempted to visualize that landscape of three centuries ago when the superintendent of this Upper Plantation, Captain Thomas Wiggin, selected this point for the home of "a considerable number of families procurred by him in the west of England, some of whom were of good estates and of some account for religion," to quote the early records, "who had crossed the sea to increase the Colony." There in 1631, sheltered by the brow of the hill, then mantled with a forest of spruce and pine, a settlement developed along the bank of the Bellamy River and in its midst a log meeting-house sufficed as house of worship from 1633 until twenty years later. Here were enacted stormy disputes between rival clergymen who for various reasons desired to control the Plantation. Among the most exciting was a riot which developed because Rev. Larkham "laid hands upon Rev. Knollys taking away his hat on pretense that he had not paid for it but he was civil enough to return it afterwards," quoting the historian, Jeremy Belknap. Again the Rev. Underhill, a third party in the strife, gathered his adherents and Rev. Knollys appeared in opposition armed with a pistol and accompanied by a band of paraders whose standard bearer displayed a Bible on a halberd for an ensign. Finally the Governor was summoned from Portsmouth who fined the offenders of the peace and banished the fighting clergy from the Plantation. Not for many years to come did the settlers of Dover enjoy the privilege of religious freedom as peacefully as they had anticipated when they sought the New World, owing to factions whose varying beliefs caused discord in the "Upper Plantation."

When prosperity began to smile because of trade in fish, furs and pipe-staves with the mother country, a framed meeting-house replaced the log hut in 1656 which was erected on the very top of the Point, surrounded by a stockade of logs set vertically, with watch towers on two diagonal corners. The Indians were beginning to exhibit alarming hostility being supplied with a quantity of fire-arms which were unlawfully purchased from the dissolute dissenters at Merry Mount in Massachusetts.

Site of the Fort Meeting-house

Eastward a few rods the log meeting-house was erected in 1633. Historically, here is the most sacred ground in New Hampshire:—the first soil to be dedicated to the worship of God in the state. The name, "Fort Meeting-house" was appropriate, truly a citadel of refuge whose foundations were so permanently laid that they remain easily traceable to this day.

Gradually the trend of growth of the plantation was directed up the river toward the waterfalls that supplied power to the saw mills. Near the close of a century of progress, a new meeting-house was necessary at Cocheco, now called Dover. In consequence, in 1760, almost a century before the state so voted, Dover separated its church from town authority. After searching all available records, the author is convinced that the statement is true that the new meeting-house was the first to be erected in the state by a church organization. It stood on the site of the present brick church and Dr. Jeremy Belknap was its famous pastor. Such is the earliest meeting-house history in New Hampshire.

50

The Oldest Meeting-house in New Hampshire
1712

COLONIAL MEETING-HOUSES IN NEW HAMPSHIRE

THE PARISH OF NEWINGTON

Passing from Dover Point over the John Sullivan bridge the road turns abruptly to the right toward the oldest meeting-house in the state. Rows of maples border the highway hemmed by rough stone walls all the way to Newington. On the right is an eighteenth century homestead, built in 1717 on land given by the parish to its first minister, Joseph Adams, an uncle of President John Adams. This nephew remarked after a visit that Uncle Joseph was "vain, loquacious, though somewhat learned and entertaining." For his day Joseph Adams was well educated, having graduated from Harvard with his A. B. and a year later with A. M. He taught school in Braintree, Massachusetts, before accepting the appointment at Newington. During the following sixty-five years, he ministered to the parish at an annual salary of thirty-one pounds and ten shillings. Whatever impression his personality may have stamped upon his nephew, when the aged minister passed to his heavenly reward the parish records read, "The Rev. Adams, our teacher, died."

In 1712, the parish of Newington separated from Portsmouth "to establish a convenient religious service." That same year a meeting-house was erected. Although the windows were holes in the walls and the seats backless benches, since the Sabbath of January 21, 1713 to the present day without interruption, a service of worship has occupied the building every Sunday under the auspices of the same organized parish society—a record which is claimed, and doubtless correctly, to be the longest in this country.

Like all colonial meeting-houses, three doors opened into the building and a belfry capped the porch on the west gable. The original bell was a gift from Newington, England, in honor of its namesake. Unfortunately, as was the habit of bells, this one cracked and was recast in 1804 for two hundred and ten dollars and the receipt was signed by Paul Revere and Sons.

The most unusual variation from the customary plans was that the east door entered into a private pew owned by the autocrat of the parish, Colonel John Downing. Only the Downing family and their invited guests occupied this exclusive sitting. When Colonel Downing died, he was buried at the northeast corner of the foundation beneath a huge slab which bears the epitaph, "This tomb built in 1739 by John Downing, Jr. age 36 yrs."

This date indicates that the tomb was prepared long before the demise of its owner. The honor of burial at the corner of the foundation of the church seems to have been a local custom around Portsmouth. Another corner-stone grave is found in Newcastle by the quaint old church although its occupant cannot be identified.

A century ago the building was remodeled. The belfry, after being struck by lightning twice on the west gable, was moved to the east and the doorway belonging to Colonel Downing became the one entrance and his aristocratic pew has since been the vestibule. The east section of the original gallery remains over the vestibule as it was built in 1712 but the other two balconies were removed and the pulpit was placed on the west side.

In the burial ground beside the church are many stones whose epitaphs are phrased according to ancient customs, including those of Rev. Joseph Adams and his family.

Most remarkable, and we believe the only relic of its pattern in the state, is a granite boulder in front of the church which bears this inscription: "After building their meeting-house, 1713, aided by thirteen yoke of oxen, the people moved this stone from the opposite field, this stone to be known as the Town Horse Block." In the illustration, the author is sitting upon the broad lower step with her back to a second on the left, like a curved stairway, which permits a person to mount easily to the top and with grace and ease take a seat upon either saddle or pillion. In the nearby town library is hanging a plan of the original floor space, each pew labelled with the family name of Pickering or Furber or one of a dozen others of colonial fame. Along the village street is seen the lean-to parsonage, built about 1700, purchased for a home for the minister after Parson Adams retired, and used now as a summertime museum. The town has continued to own the church during this last century, the janitor is paid from its taxes and the fuel is furnished from the town's forest that encloses the rear of the lot. Newington is certainly worthy of a visit; its atmosphere is historic.

The Explorers at the Town Horse Block
Collecting Historical Data

The Present Pulpit

The transition from the high colonial pulpit to the customs of the nineteenth century usually followed the course as illustrated in Newington. The sounding board was discarded and a platform occupied the space of the deacons' pew. The sacred desk, however, conformed to previous designs, the breadth was equal to the older forms.

In Exeter and Corser Hill in Webster are two examples of this transformation.

The Meeting-house at Exeter
1798

THE EARLIEST TOWNSHIPS

GREENLAND

Following the highway toward Exeter, the village of Greenland was traversed—the first parish to be separated from Portsmouth. The Congregational church displays a tablet which offers the information that the church was organized in 1706 and the building erected in 1756. Also the list of clergymen who have occupied the pulpit and dates of their pastorates is an honorable exhibit. The edifice has been so transformed from its ancient appearance that its lengthy history would not be suspected today.

MEETING-HOUSE AT EXETER

Exeter was soon entered. The ecclesiastical history of this town would fill several volumes since the day when John Wheelwright fled to its forests in 1637 after expulsion from Boston. Successive meeting-houses were destroyed before the present structure was framed in 1798. The design is noteworthy. Ebenezer Clifford from Kensington was the architect, a man who may have been acquainted with the recent innovations which the youthful Charles Bulfinch had already introduced into two churches in Massachusetts. Perhaps in the Georgian influence at Portsmouth during the previous fifty years, suggestions may have been discovered for the plans for his entire building. Whatever the source of his inspiration, Ebenezer Clifford was the first master-builder to apply Georgian patterns to a New Hampshire meeting-house. Judging from the fact that the porch is attached to the south wall, also by the position of the pillars that once supported the gallery, we conclude that Mr. Clifford took no liberties with the established order of the early interiors except the omission of two side entrances. On the exterior he worked with a free hand. No meeting-house in New Hampshire before 1798 possessed a hip-roof; also, for the first time, in place of separate doorways on three sides, triple entrances appeared on one side. The influence of Bulfinch is suspected in the detail of the cornice and the arched frames of the doors and upper story windows of the porch. Most conspicuous is the storied steeple, a forerunner of those more ornamental belfries that were to appear in the Connecticut Valley within the next fifteen years. Ebenezer Clifford deserves to be classed with his distinguished contemporary, Timothy Palmer, who is credited with the architectural grandeur of the Unitarian church in Newburyport, Massachusetts that was built six years later in 1804.

Following the usual custom, the interior has been divided at the height of the gallery and the upper story is now the auditorium. In this is a century old pulpit which should be listed with two others in the state—one at Newington and the other at Webster—their shape and detail resemble the sacred desks of the high colonial pulpits that they superseded.

In the vestibule stands a pew that was formerly a part of the Second Parish church that stood near Phillips Academy. A tablet states that President Abraham Lincoln occupied this seat when he attended a service on the Sabbath that he visited his son who was a student in Exeter. Cases filled with ancient communion plate hang from the walls of the chapel; beautiful antique chairs and tables are scattered among the several rooms for social purposes.

No other meeting-house in New England can boast of more original plans or display the creative genius of a greater master-builder. Exeter was the transition building in New Hampshire from meeting-house plans to those of the modern church of the next century.

North Meeting-house in Portsmouth
where George Washington attended a service in 1789
Erected 1712 — Razed 1856

The Church at Newcastle
with Gravestone at the Corner of the Foundation

CHAPTER VI

THE EASTSIDE MEETING-HOUSES

Like the man who believed he lived in the most favorable place in the world because he could start from his home and go anywhere, the explorers were fortunately situated in the center of New Hampshire at Plymouth. Their trips, especially those across the state to east or west, were not tediously extensive in the mileage they covered. A Sunday afternoon was selected to visit the Eastside, as the Saco Valley is named.

BARNSTEAD PARADE

Around Lake Winnepesaukee through Wolfeboro and Alton we drove to Barnstead Parade, best described in an address by Dr. John Wheeler, a native son of that town, which he delivered at the centennial celebration of the church in 1896. In explanation it may be well to state that Barnstead was one of the towns that was granted by Governor John Wentworth to a group of proprietors led by Reverend Joseph Adams of Newington, in 1727, and several villages grew to some importance in this extensive township.

Dr. Wheeler said: "How came this church building to be located at Barnstead Parade, on one side of the town, being about one mile from Pittsfield line? Because Jonathan Bunker, of Durham, a miller, mechanic, and valuable pioneer, had a lot of land here which, bounded by the Province Road, lay on both sides of Suncook river, where he had an excellent fall. He came here in 1769, and built a home on a part of his land now owned by Deacon Hiram Rand, of the fifth generation from him. He also built a saw mill and a grist mill, and had a shop with a trip-hammer, where he manufactured such iron and steel implements as new settlements required. He was succeeded by his son, Eli, who gave the site for the church and parade ground.

Barnstead Parade

"Dr. Jeremiah Jewett came here from Rowley, Mass. in 1792, and practiced medicine for forty-four years, about thirty-two years without a competitor in the whole town. He boarded with the Bunkers at first, and, being of Congregational stock, was first to move for the erection of this church. The Bunkers were good millers and brought custom from afar, because they made good flour. They were very industrious and reliable citizens and helped to uphold the church. One of the fifth generation, a successful pioneer and resident of Minnesota for nearly forty-two years, comes to us to enjoy this celebration today."

THE EASTSIDE MEETING-HOUSES

"On the first day of May, 1796, the town having been without church or minister for about twenty-nine years, since the first settlers located here, Eli Bunker furnished the following bond:

"This may certify that I, the subscriber, promise to give Charles Hodgdon, Rufus Evans, Jonathan Young, and Joseph Bunker, a committee chosen by a body of men for the purpose of erecting a meeting-house in the North part of Barnstead, as committee men for said proprietors, a deed of a piece of land for the use of said meeting-house, any time when said meeting-house is built, and a parade 27 rods by Dr. Jewett's and running back from said road so far as 25 rods towards the river, which is to be left a square for said parade; on which is not to be erected any building excepting for the use of said church, or meeting-house, any time when said committee shall demand it, which is to be free as their property so long as there is a meeting-house to stand there. As witness my hand, Barnstead, May 1, 1796, Eli Bunker. Benjamin Nutter, Benjamin Hodgdon."

"This church was commenced and finished outside, and painted yellow, with south front door and two end porches for entrance below, with stairs to reach the entrances to the galleries. A floor, temporary seats, and other arrangements were placed inside so that it was used for worship by a community that was greatly gratified by the privilege. It was thoroughly completed in 1799, and dedicated September 16, of that year.

"It had galleries on three sides, with square, paneled pews, with a rail and balusters and hinged seats on two sides in some pews and three in others, and a door which could be securely buttoned. There was an altar and a high pulpit, which was entered by a flight of stairs with two landings, through a door which the minister always buttoned carefully, as he entered. The desk was cushioned, as well as the seat, and there was a window in the rear with a half-circular top, unlike the other windows of the church. It had a large sounding-board, or rather box, above the pulpit, elaborately finished, as was the front of the pulpit, with mouldings and angles. Its attachment above seemed dubiously frail to me, and as my father's pew was well in front, I used to speculate with much anxiety about its falling on the minister's head, and bouncing over on me. The galleries were finished carefully with mouldings and supported by cylindrical pillars. The painting was dark brown. The talk about the bedlam-like tumult, for a half a minute, attending the replacing of the seats, after prayer, purposely increased by the youngsters, is nonsense. People were reverent in those days and performed the act decently and in order, with very little noise. Youngsters dared not cause confusion. If a boy wished "to cut up" he would go to the sunny-seats in the galleries, if he could get permission. But this was not always a safe place, for self-constituted tithingmen would sometimes make fierce attacks on the hair or ears of a wrong-doer. I have still a pungent recollection of my experience in those cosy seats.

"The finishing of this church, in its original form, was creditable to Richard Sinclair, who directed it, as agent or contractor. Its architectural proportions and style of finish surpassed most churches of its class in a broad circuit around it. When all things were completed, the building was placed in charge of "Uncle" Joe Bunker, a soldier of the Revolution, as sexton. He took great pride in his office, which, as there was no means of heating the house for more than thirty years, was almost a sinecure, its duties consisting of bearing a heavy key, with which he unlocked one outside door on Sunday morning, and entering, unbarred the other two, reversing the process after the afternoon service. All town-meetings were held here for twenty-four years after it was built; for the eight years following, they were held here one half the time, and for the next nineteen years, until the town hall was built, in 1847, one third of the time. Political meetings were never held here.

"In 1866 the Parade church was remodeled, belfry and bell were necessary additions and a settled minister was engaged after a long period in which the doors had not been opened on the Sabbath Day."

LEIGHTON'S CORNER MEETING-HOUSE

A few miles from Center Ossipee stands the Leighton's Corner meeting-house, approximately a century in age. Within are two relics of peculiar curiosity. Against the rear wall is a quaint choir stall, well illustrated on the opposite page. The designer of the posts for the railings must have borrowed his patterns from the spool beds of that period. Suspended by wires from the ceiling, is a sample of the inventive genius

The Choir Stall at Leighton's Corner Meeting-house

The Meeting-house at Wakefield — 1785

of a native tin-smith, a sheet iron drum to connect the two stove pipes that extend from the box stoves at the other end of the room.

Recently an enthusiastic group in the neighborhood have begun restoration to preserve this historic memorial of the early settlers.

WAKEFIELD

Northward on the Eastside Boulevard the sight of Wakefield as it spreads along the slope of the hill is picturesque. Dominating the scene is the white steeple of the one hundred fifty years old meeting-house. Although the edifice has been remodeled, fortunately the tiers of windows have been unchanged along the side walls and the porch and steeple were additions rather than modifications of the original meeting-house structure.

Unique in the state was the use to which the upper story was given for here Wakefield Academy flourished and the school room is preserved intact. Summer visitors find this an interesting place to explore.

The steeple differs from other designs in the state. The spire rises above the square belfry with tapering sections not unlike St. Bride's in London. Perchance from this likeness has arisen the rumor that the steeple is a design by Christopher Wren.

A tradition exists that the distinction of owning the oldest meeting-house in Wakefield belongs to the Congregational Society of Union, one of the villages in that township. The structure is said to have been stolen from the Piper District in 1780 and moved in one night to Union. While this tale may be pure fabrication nevertheless some consideration for its authenticity is reasonable since the custom of stealing buildings was not unknown at that period. Stories are told in several towns of school buildings that were moved in the darkness by rival districts, but school-houses of that day did not equal the dimensions of even the smallest meeting-houses. However, this myth is too important to be forgotten.

The Meeting-house at Effingham
Erected 1798 — Rededicated 1898

THE EASTSIDE MEETING-HOUSES

EFFINGHAM

The road led on through Ossipee and east to the top of Lord's Hill in Effingham. The early controversies in rival hamlets were described in an address at the rededication of the building in 1898 by the late Francisco W. Barker, from which certain facts are copied.

The town records state that on December 8, 1794 at a town meeting the vote was passed that "the meeting-house when built shall set on land at Weare Drake's." Also voted to "cut and hew timber and haul it to the spot and begin work next Monday, timber to be cut for house 36 ft. wide and 46 ft. long. Weare Drake to be a committee to oversee cutting of timber." However, not the next Monday nor for many Mondays to come did this work begin because in the village at Lord's Hill lived Isaac Lord, Esq., a selectman and enterprising citizen whose leadership challenged that of Weare Drake at Drake's Corner. The usual controversy followed. At successive meetings votes were passed in an attempt to "set the meeting-house to accommodate the whole town." Again in 1796, "To alter the setting of the meeting-house to the center of town, as near as the land will permit." A committee was chosen from other towns "to pitch on the most delightful and convenient place, nearest the center and say where said meeting-house shall set. The selectmen to provide for the committee when they think best." Two more years slipped by; then the vote was passed on March 18th, 1798, "That the meeting-house committee come and view town and prospect of settlement and upon consideration of accommodations and best advantages of the town, to say where said meeting-house shall set."

Here was the strategy of a watchful waiting. Lord's Tavern was a commodious house of entertainment where the committee was accommodated when they came to settle the dispute. Quite probable is the surmise that "the hospitality of Isaac Lord may have had some weight in influencing the committee to locate the meeting-house on Lord's Hill, almost in front of Lord's Tavern." After the building was erected, in the treasurer's accounts for the year 1800 appears the following: "March 15, paid account of Isaac Lord, Esq. for attendance, rum, and victualing committee to fix place for meeting-house in the year 1798."

TAMWORTH

Homeward through Tamworth, that most unique religious landmark was passed, Ordination Rock. On the top of a boulder approximately fifteen feet high and the same in diameter stands a monument
with a tablet that tells the story of how Samuel Hidden was ordained
there to the ministry before the settlement had erected their meeting-
house. On a lot not far from this spot a tablet preserves the site of
that first house of worship.

Only the graves of the town's fathers and mothers now guard this
sacred relic beside the highway.

CHAPTER VII

BETWEEN THE RIVER VALLEYS

HOPKINTON

Summer found the explorers surveying the area between the two principal river valleys among the foothills of the central region of New Hampshire. The entrance to this historic trail was at Hopkinton, a town just within the northern fringe of Scotch-Irish settlements in 1730, although it was not incorporated and named Hopkinton before 1765. Several hamlets gradually nestled in hollows between the hills, each convinced that it would eventually develop into the commercial center of the town.

In the beginning a settler, whose name is perpetuated at Putney Hill, built Putney's Fort in 1744 in which, for want of a better place, all public assemblies were accustomed to gather. On this hill was established the minister's lot where the parsonage of Elder Scales remains today, a dilapidated relic of 1760.

Nevertheless the town fathers did not decide to locate their meeting-house in that isolated hamlet. In 1766 a rude building was set upon the common opposite the site of the present Congregational church in the eastern outskirts of the village of Hopkinton. A visitor is immediately attracted to a tablet upon the front of this church building dated, 1789-1811. Worthy, indeed, of veneration is this ancient guardian of the gates of the city.

Early in 1789 a young minister was elected by the town and plans were adopted for a commodious meeting-house. Forthwith the temperament of the Scotch-Irish displayed its most stubborn characteristics;

71

The Meeting-house at Hopkinton
1785 — 1811

each hamlet boasted about its peculiar importance, each demanded that the building be set within its limits. Unfortunately, a youth conceived the idea that he might hasten the solution of the problem by setting fire to the existing meeting-house, on a February night. In consequence of his misdemeanor the controversy blazed with greater fury. Putney Hill, east end, and west end clamored for precedence. Two factions engaged in a free for all fight so violently did tempers overcome judgment.

A town meeting was called to convene in the tavern of Major Babson three days after the conflagration but the house proved too small for the assembled multitude and the meeting adjourned to the barn-yard, doubtless the most extensive clearing available in that winter season. To no decision did the meeting arrive. Consequently, the selection of a proper site was delegated to the selectmen of three towns: Gilmantown, Washington and Linesborough.

Meanwhile the ceremony for ordination of the young minister required immediate action. With a platform in front of the tavern as a substitute for a pulpit and all of God's out-of-doors for a temple, on February twenty-fifth—whether in sunshine or snow storm no one knows —those hardy pioneers witnessed the consecration of their minister to his holy profession.

Within the following two weeks the peacemakers reported as follows: "We your Committee appointed to fix upon a Suitable Plac in your Town for you to build a meeting hous upon, do Report that we have Taken a View of the Principle parts of your Town, and the Situation of Each Part of Same, and have found it to be attended with difficulty Rightly to Settle the matter in such a way that Each Part of the Town Should have theare Equality of Privileges." The use of capitals seems to have been employed for emphasis. After describing several sites under consideration, the committee's decision was for the same location as the burned meeting-house.

Within four months the roof of the new edifice could shelter an audience although the interior was unfurnished. The following story copied from a history of Hopkinton illustrates the customs and temperament of the Scotch families.

"One Saturday afternoon the people of the town met for the purpose of bidding off the pews. The pews were built square like so many sheep-pens with doors hung on hinges. After this a cap-piece for a finish went

73

around the top of the pews including the doors, which was securely nailed on. When a pew was sold, the carpenter would saw the cap-pieces off at the joints of the doors which gave the owner the privilege to walk in and occupy. Some of the more thoughtful ones at the meeting suggested that no person who bid off a pew should have his pew door sawed open until he walked over to Major Babson's Tavern and paid for the toddy for the company.

"At length the tallest man in the town bid off his pew. Nearly all the company spoke with one accord, "Now, it is your turn to treat." "No" said the man, who realized that too many libations had already been offered that day, "my legs are long and I can get over into my pew someway." A mischievous young neighbor assisted by a few others constructed two sets of rude stairs, one from the aisle to the top and one set down into the pew. Having heard of the work of the young jokers, the following Sabbath morning the service had already begun when the good man arrived and nearly all the hearers were in their seats. His seat was located in a conspicuous part of the house but he with his family walked up the aisle, up the stairs and down into the pew, to the no small amusement of the congregation and a smile from the parson."

Over Diamond Hill where the state highway now enters Hopkinton, in 1811, a Revere bell was drawn on an ox team and hung between two elms, a surprise to the inhabitants. Then a belfry was erected. In later years this bell was sold to a cotton factory and its subsequent history is forgotten.

The Congregational Society purchased the meeting-house in 1829, moved it from the common to its present site and remodeled it as it stands today. The clock has recorded the hours since that time.

HENNIKER

On to Henniker the search carried the explorers where a public building may be seen whose frame is that of the meeting-house of 1786, now transformed into the "town building." It was raised with the help of three barrels of rum. A vote is recorded that Dr. Hunter be paid 12 pounds, 5S., 1 and 2-4P for ninety-three gallons and a quarter of rum and three empty barrels. So Scotch was Henniker.

BETWEEN THE RIVER VALLEYS

HILLSBOROUGH

In Hillsborough everyone should pause for a call at the Franklin Pierce Homestead to admire the pictured wallpaper on the parlor, the restored frescoes, the long up-stairs ball-room and bedrooms combined, and the cosy nurseries between the pairs of east and west chimneys where in their warmth the children were cuddled in cold winter weather. No meeting-house remains in this town.

WASHINGTON

On up the hill to Washington, claiming to be the first town to incorporate under the name of the Father of his Country, the drive continued. The visitor needs no eminent citizen to describe the past glory of this truly colonial village. One should be excused if he found himself cupping his hand behind his ear as he listens to catch the sound of the horn of the stagecoach, warning children and dogs to clear the way, as the driver guides his galloping steeds around the corner to a stop before the door of the many gabled tavern, with flourishes of reins and whip and loud "Whoas." The entire street cries aloud its ancient story. An elongated common is bordered on the south side by colonial homesteads, costly in their day, that hug the sloping hill-side, their rear windows facing a view of Monadnock and the lesser peaks across the expanse of a wooded valley. Along the north side of the common is the meeting-house of 1789, beside it a more modern church, a tavern, stables, and country store, the last three attached as a unit typical of the turnpike era.

As the illustration indicates, the meeting-house green was occupied by a public auction. The potential customers were seated under the maples and bidding indifferently in response to the urgent enticements of an experienced auctioneer. Meeting a friend who was an acknowledged connoisseur on antiques, we inquired the reason of her presence and that of several well known dealers since the display seemed to be of inferior quality. "We are waiting until this junk is disposed of and then this fellow has some rare pieces for us" was the reply, thus revealing

The Town House at Washington
1789

the well understood strategy of the salesman to persuade his audience
to relieve him of a quantity of accumulated impedimenta of doubtful
value.

The "History of Washington" offers the information that its meeting-
house was raised by a carpenter named Cummings who boasted that
"Every joint he ever framed
He knew would pinch a hair."

In September, 1787, a committee was appointed to "see that the body of the house should be boarded and done workmanlike." Church Tabor and Joseph Tabor were the joiners who finished the interior. Church Tabor made the quaint pillars that support the gallery. He was born in Tiverton, Massachusetts in 1755 and died in his burning house at South Hero, Vermont at the age of eighty years. The common workmen were paid "6s. for framing; carpenters, 5s. and raw hands, 4s." Each purchaser of a pew agreed to pay "2 pounds of flax by the 5th of May as is per pound on his cash note." Such brief items reveal the financial processes of that period. The steeple was added much later.*

The Gallery Posts in Washington

* SEE PAGE 110

The Church in Stoddard

STODDARD

After exploring the village and enjoying a dinner at the Inn, the party retraced the way to the foot of the seven mile hill where two paths diverged. The antiquarian may think himself wise to drive south and climb another hill to Stoddard, famous in the early nineteenth century for its glass ovens. The old church, never a meeting-house, has lost its records, its age is unknown. The belfry is an example of several structures in this section of the state which appear unfinished. The flat top seems to be waiting for its spire to complete the intention of the town fathers since only the rim of the roof is ornamented by turret-like battlements. The interior was furnished with square pews and a balcony in the rear. Several years ago a pipe organ was purchased from a church in Cambridge, Massachusetts which is believed to have been built by the Thatcher Company in the seventeen hundreds. Tuned by Father Time, its voice is melodious like an old violin. This is probably one of the oldest instruments of its kind in this country.

LEMPSTER VILLAGE

Somewhat off the beaten track today although once upon a time a thriving village on the second New Hampshire turnpike, is the hamlet of Lempster. Yet the red painted tavern still hangs out its sign for

Lempster
1795

the accommodation of travelers, the country store offers its miscellaneous assortment of wares for sale, comfortable New England homesteads still line the village streets.

A personal interest was attached to our visit since over forty years ago while a student at Dartmouth college the author's husband taught a winter term of school here to increase his income as was then the custom of young men, the college permitting them to "make up" their classroom work in the spring. With many reminiscences as the scenes recalled them to his memory, we wandered about the streets and up and down the stairs of the old meeting-house which was unlocked and open to all who came.

The history of the town informed us that in 1767 the town was incorporated although no meeting-house was provided for another twenty years. Meanwhile Rev. Elias Fisher was ordained as preacher for the town at an out-of-doors ceremony and continued to serve the community for forty-four years.

In 1795 the meeting-house was raised, at a cost of five hundred six pounds, on a hill-side which, as time passed, proved to be too distantly removed from the trend of population. Accordingly, as in many townships, the building was taken apart, moved over a mile and re-erected with the addition of a tower and belfry. After the separation of town and church, in 1835 a Congregational church was constructed at the head of the village green, leaving the old meeting-house for the use of the town.

The second story was refinished at the gallery height and there in the upper story, school rooms were equipped after a fire destroyed the village school building. There the Dartmouth student conducted his classes during the winter months. "I little realized the importance of this place or the significance of its ownership when I taught here" said the one time school teacher. He pointed to the home where he enjoyed midnight luncheons of New England mince pie with longing for his boyhood digestion.

But the village streets seemed deserted, no familiar face greeted us, for the happy boys and girls had all scattered far and wide and only the walls of the ancient meeting-house remained to remind the returning visitor of those days gone by.

The Meeting-house at North Sutton

BETWEEN THE RIVER VALLEYS

SUTTON

After securely fastening the door and window, we drove north-ward through Sutton where three houses of worship were found, one a meeting-house of the eighteenth century, now remodeled and occupied as the village church. Sutton was unusual in the fact that north, south and center parishes divided at the beginning of the ecclesiastical controversy, each built its meeting-house. With a forested hill for a background, a more recent building at South Sutton is one of the beauty spots of the town.

The meeting-house at North Sutton was probably built about 1795 after the north and south parishes separated. The master builder was John Harvey, a craftsman of ability as his remaining doorframes prove. The pulpit was furnished with a hanging bell-dome sounding board but no other facts are recalled about the early appearance of the building. In 1870 a belfry and bell were additions. The unusual peals of this innovation aroused such fear in the herds of the farmers that the event is recorded in the history of the township.

CANAAN STREET

The town of Canaan was first settled after its incorporation in 1761. The Street is a reminder of the turnpike era, surviving with little change during the century that saw the development of the lower village after the construction of the railroad. Even earlier, in 1777 the Dartmouth College road was extended from the town to Hanover to accommodate travelers to commencements who demanded a coach road. After the Grafton turnpike traversed both villages, taverns were established every ten miles along the pike where one horse chaises crowded the drovers' ox teams in their dooryards.

During this activity a new meeting-house was begun in 1793 and completed within three years. While the interior has suffered defacement through the passing decades, relics of its former furnishings are suggestive of unusual designs by the early artisans. In the lower story may be seen the posts that support the former gallery like giant hand turned spindles and a number of slip pews serve as samples of the new styles of furniture in 1796. Above in the town hall remains a structure of doubtful origin, probably a part of the rear of a high pulpit although it has the form of a broken pediment seen in colonial doorframes.

BETWEEN THE RIVER VALLEYS

BRADFORD

Retracing the road to Henniker, our way veered to Bradford. Near the shore of Lake Massasecum, a meeting-house of doubtful age adjoins a lonely cemetery. With hesitation the explorers confess that they became somewhat expert at breaking and entering such isolated buildings when the whereabouts of the custodian of the keys could not be learned readily. This one merited such a misdemeanor. One young member of the party managed to climb over the top of a window that could be slightly lowered and unbolt the outside door. Although the desire for a photograph of the pulpit which could be seen through the window was the reason for penetrating the portals, a richer discovery rewarded our efforts. Along the side of the wall stood a rustic bier, doubtless a reproduction of those used over a period of many years to bear caskets of deceased persons to the adjacent cemetery. Long ago, before roads for carts were built and footpaths were the only means of approach to lonely farms, bearers were obliged to shoulder such burdens and walk many miles pausing, when the weight became too heavy for blistered muscles, to change sides or permit a different group to carry the rude coffin to its last resting place in the burying lot set apart by the town. Perhaps this bier may explain the family burial plots on many isolated farms in the central part of New Hampshire.

SALISBURY

On the South Road in Salisbury is situated an unpretentious structure whose history in many of its details is unusual. In 1765 it is probable that a log meeting-house accommodated the settlers of Stevenstown, the original name that was given to the grant. The public lands were laid out near the Webster Farm, now the New Hampshire Orphans' Home. Two years later about midway between the north and the south limits of the township, upon Searle's Hill—named for the first settled minister—a framed meeting-house was built that, as the records show, probably resembled the house in Danville since Stevenstown, like Danville, was settled by families from King's-town.

South Road Meeting-house

Agitation increased for a more suitable location for another meeting-house in Salisbury, the name by which the town had now been incorporated. As the years passed, disagreements increased, until the East Center, and South Villages were threatened with a civil war over this problem. The house on Searle's Hill fell into disrepair and services were held on the Sabbath in the homes of citizens where the distance was too long for their families to attend on the Hill. The condition of the public mind called for a compromise. In 1788 a group of leading men organized a Meeting-House Society. No records remain which relate by what method the Society managed to secure a vote of the town that permitted them to purchase the house on Searle's Hill. They demolished this structure and with a part of its timbers and additional new material the walls of the present Congregational church building were erected on the South Road on a lot that was presented by Captain John Webster, a cousin of Ebenezer Webster, the father of Daniel.

The following year the influential Society offered to sell their meeting-house to the town with the provision that both the Standing Order and the Antipedo-baptists be permitted to worship there. After this transaction was completed, the town finished the interior. The first signer of the Declaration of Independence, then the Governor of the State of New Hampshire, Dr. Josiah Bartlett of Kingston, purchased the first pew which he occupied when he visited his nephew, Dr. Joseph Bartlett of Salisbury.

The usual arrangement of aisles, pews and pulpit was followed with the exception that in an ancient drawing of the pulpit a bell-shaped sounding board hung from the ceiling above the high pulpit. Above the porch on the west end was a belfry in which was placed an excellent bell, cast expressly for this house, which contained twenty silver dollars contributed by the minister to improve its tone.

In 1835, the entire building was remodeled. The roof was removed, walls lowered, new windows and a modern pulpit and pews installed. The spireless steeple resembles the illustration on the Stoddard church.

On the extensive grounds of the Eastern States Exposition at Springfield, Massachusetts, in Storrow Town, is another of Salisbury's ancient churches which was purchased and moved several years ago by the founders of that reproduced New England village. The steeple and portico are additions to the original structure.

Several other towns possess edifices which were framed during the meeting-house period. The Christian church building at Hill Center is over one hundred forty years of age. North Sandwich has an ancient town-house that was built in 1793 which still preserves a part of the high pulpit and other relics of its ancient furnishings.

HEBRON

As sunset dyed Mount Kearsarge to rosy purple, the explorers turned toward picturesque Smith River Valley. On the shore of Lake New-found in Hebron was a meeting-house of 1800 raised by Benjamin Wood-man to whom the town fathers extended a vote of thanks and presented a bottle of brandy—not rum—"at the expense of the town for his generous and manly behavior while a resident of the town." Over the Mayhew Turnpike to Plymouth and home the explorers completed another his-torical drive.

The Meeting-house at Hebron

88

CHAPTER VIII

EARLY STEEPLES AND THEIR BELLS

"Build a church without a steeple!
Cussed church and cussed people."

With this couplet an irate critic in a village in Vermont expressed his opinion of the church and people—of Scotch descent, by the way—who decided not to build a steeple on their new meeting-house. These thrifty Caledonians were conforming to the almost universal idea that a steeple was useless without a bell. This conclusion was warranted in those days for raising steeples presented mechanical obstacles that were complicated to a greater or lesser degree by the amount of available apparatus to accomplish the task.

To determine the methods employed to elevate a steeple to its lofty position involves some speculation although certain facts have been gleaned from chance remarks in diaries and from records in town account books, which lead to the conclusion that the belfry and spire and all intervening members were completed on the ground and weather-vane attached. The entire steeple for a brick tower was constructed inside its walls and raised within from the floor to the height of the tower. On the contrary, because the interior of wooden towers was blocked by struts and braces, its steeple was necessarily built beside the tower, raised along the wall, and drawn back upon the platform at the top.

Tackle and falls, capstan or windlass, lifting-jack and shears were the hoisting apparatus, so constantly in use in New England's ship-yards. In Newburyport a record mentioned that all available ropes were borrowed from a neighboring ship-yard for the raising; another, farther inland, told that all the ropes from the surrounding countryside were collected at the meeting-house.

Center Church on the Green
1812

In the boyhood diary of a citizen of Connecticut was found the story that he saw the steeple of the Center Church on the Green in New Haven raised up through the brick tower with windlass and tackle in about two hours in the year, 1812.

The Meeting-house at Farmington
1771

During the discourse at the centennial celebration of the meeting-house
at Farmington, Connecticut, Noah Porter, Jr., afterward president of Yale
College, was quoted as saying that this
steeple—now standing—was "lifted to
its place along the tower walls" and was
"raised entire."

Ship Church at Hingham, Massachusetts

This is the oldest meeting-house in New England, built in 1680.

A service of worship has been held in this building every Sabbath since the day it was dedicated, although under the auspices of several separate religious societies.

EARLY STEEPLES AND THEIR BELLS

THE PURITAN STEEPLE AT HINGHAM

Doubtless the oldest steeple in New England is above the hip-roof of the "Old Ship Church" in Hingham, Massachusetts. The author has taken the liberty to distinguish this design by the name of Puritan since that sect copied this model repeatedly during the seventeenth and early eighteenth centuries. To appreciate this appropriate name, "Ship Church," one must stand on the floor of the auditorium and study the framework of the roof, as no ceiling now intervenes. The builders inverted the hull of a ship, its curved ribs becoming rafters, above the central section to form its roof. On the east and west ends additions have enlarged the auditorium and the furnishings of square pews and high pulpit are now restored according to the plan of a century and a half ago.

On the top of the roof, a truncated pyramid, is also proof of its nautical origin for a "deck-walk," like those found in seacoast towns in Maine and in Portsmouth above the homes of sea captains, was constructed for a look-off with the belfry in its center, surrounded by a balustrade for the protection of those who watched for a sight of a returning sail in blusterous weather. Above the whole is the weathervane —an actual reason for building a spire—in full view of the entire port, a signal to which anxious housewives and sailors could turn, for the primary concern of a seaport was the direction of the wind. Consequently, along the New England coast the custom was established to fix weathervanes on tall steeples above the meeting-houses. Dispersing into the hinterland, the settlers carried the habits of weather observations with them. The broad tail of the arrow at Hingham was the common design. Inland, where farmers carved their weathervanes, a cock or an ox was frequently the model, the former more often preferred. Perhaps roosters crowing at dawn, nature's alarm to summons the family to early rising, suggested the immediate morning thought to a farmer, "What about the weather?" From this oldest church in New England we now turn our attention to the "Old South" in Boston.

Old North   Old South
1723   —   Boston   —   1729

EARLY STEEPLES AND THEIR BELLS

THE OLD SOUTH IN BOSTON

The most famous steeple of the Puritan design was erected in Boston on the "Old South" meeting-house in 1729. This brick edifice stood close to Governor Winthrop's residence, in fact within the space once covered by his garden, superseding the "little house of cedar" that served as meeting-house for Boston town since 1669. This steeple included four sections: arched octagonal belfry; a wooden lantern, with small windows in each of its eight sides; a tall spire; and a weathervane. Just prior to the Revolution, Parson Prince used the lantern for his library where he retired to write his sermons. Here he preserved the manuscript of Governor Bradford's "History of the Plymouth Plantation" until the British soldiers captured the meeting-house, burned its pulpit and pews for fire-wood, and stabled their horses within its sacred walls. Fortunately the manuscript was carried to London where it reposed, forgotten, in the library of the Bishop of London during many decades. It has now been properly restored to the archives in the State House at Boston. The clock in the tower was considered his masterpiece by its maker, Gawen Brown, before 1756 and, regularly wound by trusted members of the fire department, it has ticked away the years above Washington Street to this day.

Gradually the soldiers of the Indian Wars scattered far and wide to settle tracts of land awarded to them for military service and with them, impressed indelibly upon their memories, went the picture of the steeple of the "Old South," finest then in New England. Naturally copies were erected; three can be seen today, built about 1770 at Farmington and Brooklyn, Connecticut and Amherst, New Hampshire. The latter is the oldest in the state and its builders were boys in Salem when the "Old South" was erected. On up the Merrimack Valley traveled this design as far as Campton where two examples are found.

The octagonal lantern might be called the continental belfry from the source of its design. Dating into the twelfth century such campanile are found across Europe. In Holland are symmetrical lanterns which inspired Sir Christopher Wren to plan his successive stories of his steeples. In central Russia this arched octagon has capped the towers of cathedrals for many centuries. Master builders of New England achieved equal beauty with their native white pine.

PAUL REVERE'S BELLS

The story of bells in New England is full of historical interest, especially in the connection with Paul Revere and his metal manufacturing.

Bells were cast in New York as early as 1717, and in Connecticut in 1738. A deserter from the British army named Gillimore was employed by Colonel Hobart to cast a bell in his foundry in Abington, Massachusetts in 1768. When Col. Hobart decided to retire from his business, he sent his son and a blacksmith to Boston to teach the art to Paul Revere who was then a bell ringer in Cambridge. With eight bells in Christ church which were imported from England as models, Revere began to cast bells in 1792. His first bell which now hangs in Christ church, Cambridge, was considered too sharp in tone to be entirely satisfactory. Furthermore the bell metal frequently proved too brittle to withstand the frost of a New England winter. Joseph Revere, a son, was therefore sent to England and the Continent to learn how to alloy the copper to produce a clear tone and a stronger metal. On his return, in 1804, the foundry was moved from Lynn Street, now called Commercial, in Boston, to Canton where the firm under the name of Revere and Sons continued to cast bells until 1828. Paul Revere cast a trade mark on his bells, "Revere," or "Revere and Co." or "Revere and Son," together with the year and the number of the bell. In all three hundred and ninety-eight bells were manufactured and about seventy of them are still ringing without recasting.

In 1801, Paul Revere, Jr., began to cast bells for his own profit and his bells are marked "Revere" without date or number. After Paul Revere died in 1818, the sons continued the business another ten years. Then the firm changed its name to The Revere Copper Company, ceased to cast bells but is still in existence in the possession of descendants.

Probably the oldest bell now hanging in New Hampshire is marked "Revere and Son, Boston, 1802" and is in the belfry of the town house at Milford. This bell was presented to the First Congregational Society of Milford by Perkins Nichols of Boston and was hung in the early meeting-house. In the town house at North Hampton is another bell with the trade mark "Revere and Son, Boston, 1815." Many other Revere bells were hung in the state but unless the mountings were well balanced and the nuts firmly tightened, the metal cracked and many were recast, either by the Blake Bros. Bell Co. of Boston or the Geo. H. Holbrook Bell Co. of East Medway, Massachusetts. Where other Revere bells are now found their history will be told in connection with the steeple in which they hang.

Eagle Hall, Milford

The Town-house at Hampstead
1747

EARLY STEEPLES AND THEIR BELLS

THE TOWN-HOUSE AT HAMPSTEAD

Twelve miles on foot or horseback was too wearisome a distance to travel to attend public worship or town meeting. No wonder that those courageous souls who founded their homes in the uplands of the north parish of Haverhill, Massachusetts, desired a separate parish that their taxes might support their own meeting-house and minister. In 1745 the "preparations of their substantial timbers" was begun. Then the states' boundary line was fixed and the parish was obliged to appeal to Benning Wentworth, Governor of New Hampshire, for a charter. In 1749 the town was incorporated under the name of Hampstead, derived from a town in England. Meanwhile the frame of the meeting-house was raised, covered with sawn planks, the roof completed and a pulpit and rude benches were provided. In this unfinished house, both Sundays and week days, all public gatherings assembled during the following fifty years. Frequently, at town meetings a vote would pass to continue work on the building but funds were difficult to collect and nothing came of the action.

The building became a disgrace to the town. In 1792 community spirit was aroused to repair the meeting-house. Soon clapboards and paint and a properly furnished interior appeared and a graceful steeple, replica of Hingham, was built by Colonel Thomas Reed and Abner Rogers who subscribed for two pews in part payment for their work.

Mr. Thomas Huse of West Newbury met the minister one morning and said he had noticed the new belfry. "Now you need a bell" said he. "If you will go to Brookfield to George Holbrook and speak for a bell, I will pay for it." While keeping his own counsel, the minister was not slow to act, although not until the bell was ready for delivery did he tell his secret to a carpenter who built a framework between two trees from which to suspend the gift until arrangements could be made to raise it to the belfry. Astonishment was unbounded as the ringing tones pealed among the hills of Hampstead. Everyone rushed to see what their ears could not convince them to believe. In solemn warning they read the inscription around the neck of the bell:

The living to the church I call
And to the grave I summons all.

On one side was inscribed the legend: Presented by Thomas Huse, Esq. 1809. The other side bears the trade mark, "Revere, Boston." The bell was deeded to the town for use in civil matters, funeral occasions and in particular for the use of the Congregational Church and Society forever. Its price was six hundred dollars; its weight, 1,212½ pounds. It was raised in 1809 and has been in use over a century and a quarter. These details are of historical importance if the manufacturer is to be identified. The trade mark indicates that the son of Paul Revere probably cast the bell in his foundry which he operated in 1809; furthermore the absence of a date also bears testimony to this origin for Paul, Jr. was not accustomed to date his bells or inscribe a number upon them. The Hampstead bell does not appear on the list of Paul Revere and Sons in records that are doubtless correctly copied.

In 1820 an attempt was made to introduce a stove, and two dollars and eighty-five cents were subscribed toward its purchase. Two years after a clumsy box stove stood directly in front of the pulpit, its top covered by a pan which held about six quarts of water because "some were afraid the infernal thing would blow up." No chimney was constructed, instead the stovepipe was passed through the ceiling, then branched in two directions and outlets were made through the east and the west windows.

The last chapter in the history of the building as a house of worship was told in the sermon that was delivered on October fourteenth, 1837 by Rev. John Kelly, pastor during a ministry of forty-four years, at the farewell service of the "Standing Order" within its walls. A new Congregational church had been erected in the valley, the old meeting-house was to be left to the peaceful possession of several sects that had claimed their share of the Sabbath hours. Sad, indeed, was Parson Kelly as he admonished his listeners, "I beseech you, let there be no unhallowed feelings arise in your hearts against other denominations or individuals living in the world." Again he urged the beloved young men, "Be ye sober minded, devout, humble, serving the Lord. Let not the pleasant village of Hampstead be anything like a scene of coarse ribaldry, noise of strife. Fall not in with clownish, and illiberal manners of the times. Avoid stimulating ailments. Touch not, taste not, handle not the poisonous cup, nor noxious weed of the South . . . You may be glad to leave this house and go to a new one, but think, oh think, that you must go one step further! To prepare for this, see that you seek a house not made with hands, eternal in the Heavens."

At length, in 1852, the town took entire possession of its meeting-house, removed the pulpit and pews, built a floor at the height of the gallery and utilized the space for the business of the town. Hampstead can claim the possession of the oldest public building in New Hampshire, 1745-1938—and a steeple that is now the only one of its design in the Granite State.

IN THE PARISH OF EAST DERRY

The one settlement in the colony of New Hampshire which was established by religious refugees, was at Londonderry in 1720. These emigrants were descendants of Puritans who fled to northern Ireland in the seventeenth century to escape persecution in Scotland, only to find their contacts with the Irish of the Catholic faith were even more disastrous. After a century of conflict, these Scotch-Irish, as they were known in New England, emigrated to several grants of land in the colonies of Maine, New Hampshire, and Massachusetts.

As the colony in Londonderry increased in population, separate villages were formed, among them the East and the West Parishes. In 1769, the East Parish erected a new meeting-house which was "one of the neatest in a country of beautiful sanctuaries" says Rev. Edward L. Parker, the historian of Londonderry. "Meeting-houses were constructed to suit, in some degree, the existing state of society. The construction of the pulpit and its appendages, in Presbyterian communities, corresponded with the form of ecclesiastical government."

Accordingly in the Parish of East Derry, the deacons' seat was elevated six inches above the floor in which sat a venerable deacon at either end of the bench, facing the audience. Immediately behind and twelve inches higher, was a larger pew to accommodate the elders of the session, a dozen or more dignified brethren whose responsibilities were weighty and vested with authority. Above these two pews stood the pulpit against the north wall. Few towns under the Congregational Platform elected elders; consequently a pew for these dignitaries was unnecessary.

The Parish of East Derry — 1769

EARLY STEEPLES AND THEIR BELLS

The meeting-house was sixty-five by forty-five feet in dimensions and a steeple was also one of its distinctions, by which it "equaled if it did not surpass, in appearance, most of the edifices of that period." Deacon Daniel Reynolds and Joseph Morrison were the "undertakers" of the work. Their edifice sufficed until 1824 when more space was required. These thrifty Scotch resorted to the plan of sawing the frame through the center of the north and south walls, moved the rear section twenty-four feet and filled in the intervening space, with the original frame "as firmly joined as ever." Again in 1845 interior changes afforded an auditorium in the upper story and a spacious town hall, a vestry, a room for the sessions of the elders and a parish library on the lower floor. This was the period when pews were turned about to face the entrances and Derry followed the style. In the store-room may be seen, to this day, the semi-circular front of that pillared pulpit like the illustration in the church in Newbury.

At present, the canny Scotch inheritance is displayed by the congregation. Rather than turn the pews around and change the location of the pulpit, a rear doorway accommodates the worshipers. No longer are the front doors in the tower the entrances, instead they face a spacious green unmarked by footpaths while the entrance walk and drive are at the rear of the church and convenient for everybody.

During the changes of 1824, a new steeple was considered favorably. Although historically interested citizens have searched for the name of the carpenter who executed the design of the present steeple, at present their efforts have proved in vain. At Newburyport and in Boston, inspiration could be found for the plans of the octagonal lantern above the belfry but the design of the entire upper members must have been the artistic creation of an unknown Scotch artisan. This lantern is ornamented with fluted pillars, projecting from the angles of the walls, each capped by a canopy surmounted by a hand-turned urn at least four feet in height. No other member of a steeple in the state surpasses its craftsmanship, its classic order, no doubt, inspired by the pattern books of Palladio and Inigo Jones.

On page five is a picture of the ancient cemetery where the first settlers of the parish sleep. According to Scotch customs, all the head-stones are set at the east end of the graves and, on many of them, the inscription is engraved on the face next to the lot rather than toward the pathway between the headstones.

Situated a few miles off the beaten track, few travelers up or down the state highways ever view this ancient edifice. However, a short semi-circular detour by side-roads leads through this colonial village, where also is Adams Female Academy, the place where Mary Lyon first practiced her profession as a teacher of young women.

Within the vestry of the church are to be seen the pine panels of the original wainscoting. The bell is another interesting relic of the past, inscribed:

THIS BELL WAS BEQUEATHED TO THE

FIRST PARISH IN LONDONDERRY

BY MR. JACOB ADAMS THE FOUNDER

OF ADAMS FEMALE ACADEMY

A. D. 1822 RECAST 1824 AGAIN RECAST 1860

BY HENRY N. HOOPER & COMPANY BOSTON

CHAPTER IX

STORIED STEEPLES

The storied steeples found in the Connecticut Valley in New Hampshire and adjacent sections of Massachusetts were the valedictory of colonial craftsmen. To trace the origin of their designs it is necessary to briefly review a list of influential architects who impressed their successors with the beauty of their art during the sixteenth and seventeenth centuries; not only by the structures that they built; but, to a greater degree, by the publication of their designs in "pattern books."

A persistent myth pervades New England that its storied steeples are the genuine creations of Sir Christopher Wren. While it is true that Wren originated a fundamental element in the evolution of the structure of storied steeples, experts are convinced that this English architect has received honor beyond his just right and other men have been deprived of recognition which they deserved, in the United States.

PALLADIO

In the middle of the sixteenth century at Vicenza in Italy, 1518-1580, lived Palladio who, his biographer says, "Discovered the true rules of art which all in his time were unknown." Palladio published books containing his own designs and measured drawings of antique fragments that he found in the ruins of Roman temples and arches, which in successive editions remain highly valuable reference works for architects. From the inspiration he caught from the triumphal arches at Rome it is supposed that Palladio drew his idea for the arched, triple doorways and windows that perpetuate his name.*

* PAGE 134 AND 139

105

COLONIAL MEETING-HOUSES IN NEW HAMPSHIRE

INIGO JONES

To Inigo Jones, 1573-1652, first English architect, is due the honor of translating the Italian orders, emphasized by Palladio, for the world. It is written that Jones possessed a "born eye" for correct proportions and dimensions, "everything must be drawn to scale." What Boswell was to Johnson in literature, Jones was to Palladio in architecture. Not until late in his life was Jones' ability recognized in his native land where his patronymic was almost obliterated by the use of his nickname, Palladio, which his devotion to his master earned, perhaps in derision, from his contemporaries. A debt of gratitude is owed to Inigo Jones for the pattern books that he published containing measured drawings of his own and his predecessor's designs.

SIR CHRISTOPHER WREN

Sir Christopher Wren, 1632-1723, was influenced by Jones and his Italian background. In his youth Wren became a teacher of mathematics and astronomy in Cambridge University while he also dabbled in architecture. He had already constructed several buildings when the plague in London sent him, with many other men fleeing to Paris in 1665. At this period the Renaissance was at its height and many of the important public buildings and palaces were in process of construction permitting Wren an opportunity to observe principles of their foundations and framework as well as exterior embellishments. Returning to London with increased knowledge of techniques, gained in less than a year, the young scientist found opportunity for his creative ideas when the great fire in London devastated a square mile of the city in 1666. Immediately Wren submitted his plans for reconstruction of the burned area which brought to him a command from the king that he rebuild its fifty-three parish churches.

Steeples were then cones or pyramids, of metal or masonry, whose weight was supported on the walls of their towers. Through his knowledge of mathematics and his genius for comprehending the laws of physics, Wren was able to devise methods of bridging the void of the tower over which no architect had ventured to build. Either by a core of masonry within the tower as in St. Bride's, or by a semi-elliptical dome above the void as at St. Mary le Bow, Wren relieved the stress on the walls of the tower. Thus, massive, successive "lanterns," with graduated diameters, ascended to any desired height. The many storied steeple was a discovery and an innovation by Sir Christopher Wren.

COPIED FROM — "CHRISTOPHER WREN, HIS LIFE AND WORKS"

Above is a composite drawing of the famous steeples that Sir Christopher Wren designed. On the left center is the seven storied tower of St. Bride's, the inspiration for James Gibbs; most famous, perhaps, of all the patterns that Wren introduced. Balancing this on the right, is the steeple of St. Mary le Bow, considered to be the finest that Wren produced and named from the bows beneath the foundations of the church, relics of a much older structure. Charles Bulfinch found many suggestions here for his steeple at Lancaster, Massachusetts. In the background is the dome of the Cathedral of St. Paul, the masterpiece of this architect. No steeple in New Hampshire is a copy of a design by Sir Christopher Wren.

COLONIAL MEETING-HOUSES IN NEW HAMPSHIRE

JAMES GIBBS

A student of Wren's technique was another Englishman, James Gibbs, 1680-1754, who introduced storied steeples into the United States in 1752 with his design for St. Michael's Episcopal church in Charleston, South Carolina, patterned after Wren's St. Bride's in Fleet Street in London. Gibbs was the designer of two famous churches in London, St. Martin in the Field and St. Mary le Strand, which have been the models for many of the finest steeples in New England. Joseph Brown patterned the First Baptist Church in Providence in 1771 after St. Martin in the Field and Peter Banner, another English architect, did likewise for Park Street steeple in Boston in 1809 although the capitals of its fluted columns were achieved by a Bostonian, Solomon Willard. In 1728, James Gibbs also published several pattern books including his own designs and those of Wren and his predecessors. To many pattern books in the hands of country carpenters in New England must be attributed the masterpieces of colonial architecture. Three or four authors sufficed: a book of Palladio's designs, Pain's House Carpenter, and Benjamin Ware's Body of Architecture were commonly included in a library.

In the curriculum of every college were major courses on architecture which were considered an important factor in every graduate's equipment for life. Such men in association with their housewrights drew the plans for their own homes and, in the same manner, it is safe to presume that they acted upon committees which were appointed by the voters in the towns, to build meeting-houses. These committees conferred with carpenters, joiners, sawyers, and wood carvers in planning buildings with distinctive and individual differences although they copied a general plan from town to town. Thus it is interesting to compare a simple structure as in Danville with those in the Connecticut Valley which were built sixty years later. Regrettable, indeed, is the fact that the names of those obscure craftsmen, artists in white oak and pine, are unrecorded. Strangely, records of the town have been frequently lost, burned, or even intentionally destroyed. Careful research has failed to reveal accurate knowledge of early craftsmen. However, some slight results have accrued in our perusal of all available material and names are included wherever it is possible.

108

STORIED STEEPLES

CHARLES BULFINCH

The man who exerted the greatest personal influence was the first New England architect, Charles Bulfinch. He was born in Boston in 1763, scion of a wealthy family, his father and grandfather both skilled physicians and his mother the richest woman in Boston, in her own right. After graduation from Harvard, as was customary, Bulfinch went abroad to complete his cultural education. Two years at Oxford convinced him that architecture would become his career. Wandering about the continent, studying, and observing in the schools of famous architects filled two more years. At the age of twenty-three, equipped with an extensive technical library, Bulfinch returned to practice his profession in Boston. Many distinctive motives were productions of his pencil: arched recessive panels in walls like those of the State House in Boston; fan windows in gables; and, most important of all for our subject, the transformation of the plans of colonial meeting-houses to churches as we know them today. In 1789 Bulfinch built a church at Taunton and another at Pittsfield in 1793, both showing radical changes in their architectural plans. Now the pulpit was placed on a shorter side, doors were in the wall opposite the pulpit, aisles between slip pews extended lengthwise of the auditorium and a porch almost as broad as the front of the church contained the vestibule in which were stairways to the galleries and the roof of this porch partially supported the steeple. This complete change from the ancient meeting-house was approved everywhere.

ASHER BENJAMIN

About this time, 1790, Asher Benjamin began to publish in Greenfield, Massachusetts, his series of five books of measured drawings which contained plans for meeting-houses. He was a practicing architect who "fitted familiar forms to the needs of the time." Few of the designs which he printed are his original works; many were drawn directly from Bulfinch. The five books were widely circulated. Scores of steeples were built during the first twenty years of the nineteenth century which were copies of Asher Benjamin's measured drawings.

The Asher Benjamin Steeple
Ashby, Massachusetts
1809

Throughout Connecticut and Massachusetts and northward in New Hampshire to Washington this design was repeated on scores of churches.

The Elias Carter Steeple
Templeton, Massachusetts
1811

Northward into New Hampshire this design
was repeated along the Connecticut Valley.

The Town-house at Fitzwilliam — 1817

THE TOWN-HOUSE AT FITZWILLIAM

Thomas Stratton assisted in drawing the plans which were copied from Templeton, Massachusetts.

The Portico at Fitzwilliam

TOWN-HOUSE AT FITZWILLIAM

The portico has many points of interest: the triangular corbels in the cornice, the carved Ionic capitals.

ELIAS CARTER

In Brimfield, Massachusetts, in the year 1804, Elias Carter, "a country carpenter," built a meeting-house which is described in the history of Brimfield as having "columns in front, a very respectable looking steeple and the entrances all at one end now." Mr. Carter "went up on the gallery girth of the west side of the frame at the raising to prove his work" as was the custom. This new building was so respected by the citizens that several votes were passed in the town meeting: "that no one be allowed to go into the pulpit during town meeting nor transact any private concarns in the place of meeting;" "that it be recommended to the proprietors of pews to procure sand-boxes for their pews;" "no person should get on top of the pews during town meeting or interrupt the moderator."

Mr. Carter was but twenty-four years of age when he planned and constructed the meeting-house in Brimfield. He was born in Auburn, Massachusetts on May 30, 1781, the son of Timothy and Sarah Walker Carter. His father and uncle, Benjamin Carter, were partners in a firm of contractors. When Elias was three years old, Timothy Carter was killed by a fall from a meeting-house that he was building in Leicester, Massachusetts. Benjamin removed to Vermont and the widowed mother with her six children went to live in the vicinity of Barre, Massachusetts.

Where Elias Carter received his preparation for his profession as an architect is a mystery. Doubtless, he inherited his father's plan books and it is known that he possessed his pattern book that was published in London in 1756 by Battey Langley, called "The City and Country Builder's and Workman's *Treasury of Designs*—according to Andrea Palladio—with rules for working all the varieties of designs" as quoted from the title page. For a brief period, Mr. Carter lived in Georgia where he acquired a southern style that influenced his subsequent designs. Porticoes appear in his plans for both meeting-houses and residences. He was the architect for the meeting-house in Templeton, and the creator of the design for its storied steeple which was copied repeatedly along the Connecticut Valley in New Hampshire. Simplicity marked all of his work. He omitted the fluted pillars which ornament the angles of the octagonal lanterns that were designed by Wren and Gibbs. Instead, he employed an effect of pilasters whose capitals are incorporated in the mouldings beneath the decks of the several stories of his steeples. He introduced the Palladian window into the front wall of the second story beneath the ceiling of his portico and the oval window in the gable of the porch. By 1820 he had built twelve meeting-houses. In the church at Mendon, Massachusetts, stands a hand-carved pulpit which he executed at night after the other workmen had departed, probably dreaming its designs by candle light. His grand-daughter states "He undoubtedly commenced his career as a master-builder, later leaving the easier work to others and becoming himself the architect and wood-carver of the firm." He excelled in carving small wreaths of roses or an anthemium design for the ornamentation of his interiors. His grand-son recalls "a large collection of special planes, twenty or thirty in number, by which he could make mouldings of different designs." On the front wall of the Templeton meeting-house are three panels, two ovals and a central rectangle, which are probably examples of his exquisite carvings. He preferred plain shafts for his pillars with carved volutes of the Ionic order in their capitals. He kept up with the times, however, and in later life adopted the prevailing classic style of the Greek Revival. Elias Carter died in Chicopee Falls in 1864, leaving New Hampshire and the Connecticut Valley deeply indebted to his skill and creative genius.

THE TOWN HOUSE AT FITZWILLIAM

The influence of Elias Carter entered New Hampshire at Fitzwilliam, a town that borders on Massachusetts not many miles north of Templeton, and of Athol, Massachusetts.

Although the town voted to build in 1803, disagreements prevented actual construction until 1816. In Norton's history of the town is found the statement that Thomas Stratton was paid three dollars and thirty cents to assist the committee in drawing the plans. Because this is the only record known to the author where a draftsman's fee was paid to a citizen every effort has been made to discover to what extent Thomas Stratton collaborated. Several residents of Fitzwilliam have given valuable assistance in this research. Mrs. Howard M. West visited neighboring towns, especially Templeton, but to no purpose. The town clerk and the historically minded selectman, Lewis Webb, have perused old records for a possible clue.

One August afternoon a visit was arranged to the Fitzwilliam town building where Mr. Webb disclosed his findings in tax books of 1815-1818, composed of yellowing paper, lined into columns with lead pencil and captioned at their top with property, school, minister and other taxes. The name of Thomas Stratton appeared among those who paid the highest amounts proving that he was possessed of considerable wealth. In 1817 his name disappears and Thankful Stratton paid the taxes the following year and then her name disappears also. Since the name, Stratton, was not found in the list of original families in Fitzwilliam, the census of 1790 was consulted. In the town of Athol, Massachusetts, Thomas Stratton was found and the date when he married Thankful Rich. He was born there in 1758, fought in the Revolutionary War, became town clerk in 1788. "He carefully kept the records and his fine penmanship is shown by the old town records" was a testimonial discovered in the Stratton Genealogy. He also served as selectman, treasurer and representative to the legislature in successive terms of years. Then, in 1812 he sold his property in Athol and removed to Fitzwilliam. His reputation must have been high for he immediately became selectman in his new home and representative in the New Hampshire legislature. He was killed in 1818 by a falling tree.

In a diary written by Benjamin Hubbard of Rindge we learn that the edifice was dedicated on November twenty-sixth, 1816. After three months of use this same diary states—"January 17, 1817. A storm from the South East with Lightning and thunder which commenced about two o'clock at Night with Rain and Hail. Fitzwilliam Meeting House Burnt by Lightning Which took fire in shavings under the house." To emphasize this entry a drawing of a hand with five fingers extended toward this item adorns the margin of the page.

From Norton's history may be learned that "the pulpit Bible was saved by Jonas Roberson while flames burst from the doors and windows." Unfortunately all the debris left by the carpenters had been swept into the cellar which furnished dry kindling for the sparks from the lightning to quickly consume. The catastrophe was widely deplored. In Ashby, where we have seen another fine meeting-house, built in 1809, the fellow feeling of sympathy was such that fifty dollars was voted in a town meeting to Fitzwilliam "on account of the loss of their church by lightning."

In the diary of Mr. Hubbard is found at a latter date "June 6th, 1818. Fitzwilliam began to raise a New Meeting House and finished today, Election Day." In the margin is a note surrounded by a circle "See other being burnt." It is recorded that the entire population of the town united to rebuild the meeting-house which was completed in a year and four months.

Mr. Webb introduced an aged citizen to us, William Elisha Barcas, who from boyhood attended Sabbath worship with his grandmother and recalls tales he heard from her lips that are more than a century old. When asked if the new building copied the former, in emphatic tones came the reply, "Exactly, exactly." He described the arrangements of the interior saying that the pulpit was like those of that period, probably resembling Exeter. The pews were slip design with doors; stoves stood in the rear and the pipes extended the length of the auditorium; the choir sat in the rear gallery and the audience arose and turned to face the singers during the hymns. Galleries were built on three sides with stairways in the vestibule.

The village of Fitzwilliam consists of numerous colonial homesteads. Mr. Barcas recalled Deacon Spaulding who resided next door to the meeting-house. Loving children, Deacon Spaulding was accustomed to fill his wagon with as many youngsters as it could possibly accommodate and allow them to take turns driving his trusty horse. The deacon also possessed a small pet dog that accompanied him wherever he went, except to church. One June Sabbath the boy, William, was sitting with his grandmother when he saw this dog enter the deacon's pew and jump upon the seat just as the long prayer was about to be offered by the minister. The dog reverently faced the pulpit and sat in dignity throughout the prayer and sermon. From that day to the end of his life this faithful friend sat beside his master on the Sabbath. Such were memories of a boyhood, now eighty years past and gone.

In the beginning the lot was a present to the town; strangely after the fire the price of one hundred dollars was demanded for some forgotten motive. A mile from the site was the Sally Kendall place where the oak and pine timbers were cut from her woodlots; Samuel Kendall was the master builder. One interesting story of the portico relates that the logs for the pillars were drawn to the site to be turned there into columns and their centers bored from end to end to prevent cracks. Each column has a rectangular opening, for some unexplained reason, about half way up the shaft. After years of weathering, their bases decayed explaining the presence today of chamfered granite blocks for supports.

The original Revere bell, in the key of A, fell during the fire without harm and was replaced in the new belfry only to be cracked years after when the ringer became too vigorously excited because a fire was destroying one of the largest homesteads in town. With the hope that its tones would be more like the ringing of silver, three hundred silver dollars were contributed by the farmers to be added to the recast metal. An inscription contributes to the history of foundries, "Cast by Wm. Blake & Co., Formerly N. H. Hooper & Co., Boston, Mass." The Seth Thomas clock was not purchased until 1870.

It is the boast in the town that the ridge pole is one pine timber sixty-six feet in length, its curved side cradled in a cavity hollowed in the top of the foot square, oak king posts. The steeple posts are oak also; the entire framework demonstrates the mighty forests of primeval days.

Until 1856 public worship was united under this roof, although harmony had not prevailed between various factions. Finally the Baptists and Congregationalists reluctantly relinquished their rights leaving the Unitarians in possession of the meeting-house. In 1868 the upper floor was laid; the interior space was utilized for many purposes until today all of the semblance of its former religious aspects have disappeared from the "Town House."

THE TOWN MEETING-HOUSE AT JAFFREY

A few miles across a ridge of hills from Fitzwilliam is a meeting-house in Jaffrey that resembles Sandown as it should since it was erected at the same period, 1774. The contrast between the flashes of wars and rumors of wars heard over the radio today, and that "time that tried men's souls" can be appreciated if thought is given to the quiet contentment in towns then several days' journey from the seat of the colonial government at Portsmouth and the seashore where the enemy were certain to commence their attacks. Imminent war disturbed but slightly the village of Jaffrey, rather the new meeting-house was the topic of discussion in town meetings with the decision finally reached to build like the house in Rindge.

At a most critical moment the appointed day for the raising arrived, June seventeenth, 1775. Two barrels of rum were purchased to increase the jollity of the occasion with the expectation that the events would occur according to the usual schedule. Suddenly an ominous reverberation rolled to the ears of the company. Again and again this unusual muffled report kindled astonishment, then aroused fear. Cannon and only cannon could cause this disturbance. Joy turned to gloom at the raising in Jaffrey and justly so since fourteen sons of the town had already joined the troops under John Stark's command around Boston.

While this tale may seem mythical, skeptical investigators have become convinced that over the seventy miles of air line as the crow flies between Boston and Jaffrey, vibrations did pass as the record from town to town repeats this story. The historian of Jaffrey, the late Albert Annett, vouches for the truth of this tradition. The heavy artillery on the British warships was the probable cause of the violence of the sound waves, according to Mr. Annett. Again, in other sections of New Hampshire are recalled the testimonials of farmers, trained in the skills of Indians, who caught the vibrations of the guns at Bunker Hill over nature's telephone—by placing theirs ears to the ground—in Hanover, Campton and Plymouth.

Mr. Annett verified another tradition of the history of meeting-houses: that experts assisted local carpenters. So, in Jaffrey, while the timbers for walls were framed by local men, three housewrights were brought from Georgetown, now Bradford, Massachusetts: Jeremiah Spofford, and his son, Jacob Spofford, and Jacob Haskell, to frame the roof. The name of Spofford has been mentioned in company with Timothy Palmer at Rocky Hill in 1789. Probably this Jeremiah was born in Rowley, Massachusetts, then moved to Bradford where he engaged in lumber business and carpentry. His sister was the wife of the chairman of the building committee in Jaffrey. The family is found at Newburyport and Daniel Spofford and Ambrose Palmer furnished the lumber of the Unitarian church which Timothy Palmer built, in 1804.

That these Spoffords were experts has been proved by time. So

121

firmly were the joints of their king post trusses fixed that when this meeting-house was restored ten years ago, the architect, Mr. Cann of Jaffrey, found the heavy cross-beams slightly crowned exactly as they were set, a custom that was intended to wedge the frame all the more closely if any settling of the ceiling timbers should occur.

The town was obliged to postpone completion of the interior until after the close of the war. Finally fluted pillars supported the paneled balcony and a high pulpit stood on the north wall and the pews were finished with "Banisters" by order of the voters. Also porches covered the east and west doorways.

After the Toleration act was passed, in 1822 the voters decreed that each denomination should use the town-house on Sabbath days for worship in proportion to the valuation of the property that each possessed, a fair proposition. Meanwhile in the progressive towns surrounding Jaffrey, steeples were rising heavenward. Again the voters decided that a belfry might be built by subscription by "Individuals" at the west end. In a letter from Mrs. Abby A. Day of Jaffrey who cooperated in our research, the name of the architect or country carpenter as he was called by Mr. Annett, was recorded. Joel Oakes Patrick, born in 1793, the son of a carpenter, "was a natural draughtsman and a scholar." He became a merchant and hotel keeper but "lacked that capacity for business which means financial success." He left Jaffrey the richer, however, with several structures: the Butler House, a store with unusual cornices, a barn on the Prescott Place called a masterpiece of framing; and the steeple like a pattern of lace-work, with proportions that certainly adorn the porch on the quaint old meeting-house. A Revere bell was immediately purchased at a price of $440.30, which cracked and was recast by Henry N. Hooper Company of Boston.

After 1844, the building ceased to be occupied for religious worship, fell into dilapidation and the pulpit and pews, balcony and pillars were destroyed and forgotten. Concern was felt by some citizens causing John Conant, Esq. as far back as 1872 to present to the town almost a thousand dollars to become the nucleus for a fund to repair the meeting-house. After years, the Village Improvement Society, in 1926, restored the interior. Mr. Cann discovered fragments of the original pillars and panels for patterns for the new balcony and a roomy stage fills the space where the pulpit once reared its sounding-board.

The Paul Revere Bell at Hancock
1820

In the accounts of Paul Revere and Son this bell
is recorded as number 236, September 13, 1820, weight
1,166 pounds.

The Town-house at Jaffrey
1774

THE TOWN-HOUSE AT JAFFREY

This building was erected in 1774; the steeple was designed by Joel Patrick, a citizen of the town; and raised to the top of the tower in 1823.

The Attic at Jaffrey

THE ATTIC AT JAFFREY

A comparison with other illustrations will show that the same principles for roof timbers were employed throughout New England before the Revolution:—king post trusses and double rafters.

MOUNT MONADNOCK FROM THE BELFRY

In our introduction hill-tops were mentioned. The surroundings of Jaffrey's meeting-house fulfil the ideal—crowning the summit of a gently sloping elevation; the ancient cemetery in its rear; a spacious green in front, scattered with maples; and the overshadowing background of rugged Mount Monadnock. If any spot deserves the name of shrine, this old white landmark is worthy to be thus dedicated.

The Corbeled Lintel above the
Crucifixion Doors at Hancock

HANCOCK

Further north, a few miles, another steeple of this group appears
over the tree-tops at Hancock. Not as historic as Jaffrey's, because it
replaced the meeting-house of 1789 which was destroyed by fire in 1819,
leaving Hancock destitute of any place for public assembly. The following year occurred the raising which required two days "before the
ridge-pole was wet down with a bottle of rum." The pew space was

sold at an auction, which brought seven thousand dollars, a sum sufficient to erect the entire building. The committee appointed to supervise the plans was instructed to follow the design of Dublin's meeting-house, since demolished. It is recorded that Dublin copied Fitzwilliam, a fact readily believed when Hancock's steeple is compared with the latter.

Like a will-o-the-wisp a vague impression has occasionally been sensed that "a portico was not considered in good taste" for a meeting-house, an idea with flavor reminiscent of the puritanical severity of the forefathers. Porches conformed to the religious pattern. Likewise, triple doorways, connected by a horizontal lintel, were considered to represent the Trinity; the Father, the Son and the Holy Spirit.

The importance of such distinctions can be clearly understood by descendants of that resolute stock that participated in the bitterness engendered by disputes over doctrinal dogmas. Whether a belief in Unitarian tenets was or was not a conviction for eternal damnation depended upon which ground our progenitors worshiped.

Hancock was orthodox. Its triple doorways, adorned with a wealth of hand carving, plainly proclaimed to all passers-by the religious principles of the community.

In 1820, the town purchased a Revere bell cast in the foundry of Joseph Revere, son and successor of Paul Revere who died in 1818. Apparently the metal that Joseph learned to prepare in England where his father sent him for investigation, proved satisfactory, his bells have endured the frost of over a hundred winters.

In 1851, this building was moved to its present site, modernized with an auditorium in the upper story and the town's hall below, a union of Congregational church and town that persists in only one other place in the state at present: Rindge.

No more beautiful picture can be found at evening throughout New England than Hancock's white steeple gleaming in the glare of flood-lights against its background of dark forest if the privilege of driving along the valley of the Contoocook river is vouchsafed by kindly good fortune.

131

The Congregational Church at Hancock
1820

THE CONGREGATIONAL CHURCH
COMBINED WITH THE
TOWN HOUSE AT HANCOCK

The steeple is a copy of Fitzwilliam but Hancock was orthodox, the town fathers preferred a porch in place of a portico.

The Porch at Hancock

THE PORCH AT HANCOCK

The detail on this front is remarkable; — in
the lintel of the triple doors, the hoods in the
Palladian window, the caps of the pilasters, and
corbels above the clock face.

The Puritan Steeple
of the Merrimack Valley

The Storied Steeple
of the Connecticut Valley

STORIED STEEPLES

ACWORTH

When John Stark led his colonial troops across from Boscawen to Fort No. 4, now Charlestown, in the days of the French and Indian Wars, the trail traversed Acworth. In time this pathway became the first "coach road" in New Hampshire. If its windings are followed to the summit of Acworth Village, a reward will amply repay the ascent. Set upon the highest elevation of all meeting-houses in the state, this beautiful church is considered by experts in colonial architectural design, to be the culmination of complete art in white pine.

Unfortunately few records can be discovered to indicate whether town or church, perhaps both, were responsible for its construction. In 1814, it was recorded that the roof of the old meeting-house was so punctured with holes that during a Sabbath worship the audience room was "completely flooded" by a severe thunder shower. Nevertheless disputes among the various denominations prevented repairs. At length an agreement was reached to build a new church, probably by vote of the town, for the provision was exacted that from the timbers of the old meeting-house, a town building should be erected. This was accomplished in 1820. The "town-house," church and a gift to the town, a modern school-house, now stand side by side along the village common.

A comparison with the designs of Fitzwilliam and Hancock will be convincing evidence that Acworth was the creation of another craftsman. That the forgotten hand that held the pencil was an artist of rare ability is proved by the fact that he did not cap his steeple with a spire as the other storied examples display. For a building that has only the sky for a background, the "dish cover" design, as it was appropriately named long ago in England, was most fitting. How like the top of grandmother's sugar bowl this metal cap piece is curved. Words cannot do justice to the beauty, rather a visit of several hours is necessary to perceive, to any degree, the wealth of detail in the handiwork of skilled wood-carvers that is lavished upon the exterior.

A few points should be emphasized. In all three steeples the balustrades should be noted for each is a different and simpler design from lantern to lantern. Everywhere this same custom was followed in balu-

137

strades. Spirelets decorate the corners of two towers; graceful urns are repeated at scores of points. The corbels in the detail of the cornices should be noted—a triangular design that originated in New England, perhaps a creation of Bulfinch as it is not found before his works appear. The Palladian windows and the ovals supported by carved olive branches, the Ionic capitals on pilasters or pillars and the variation of their bases are all full of interest. The simplicity of the pilasters that form the angles of the arches of the octagons on the lanterns are the most original distinctions of these steeples as comparison with all others in New England will prove. The weathervanes are identical and their weight is almost unbelievable. Several years ago a cultured woman returned from years of educational service in Boston to her native Acworth. To her dismay she discovered that the metal covering at the top of the steeple was so rusted that moisture was seeping through and would in time reach to the foot square oak beams that support the steeple. After collecting all the funds she was able to solicit she drew upon her own bank accounts for the necessary remaining hundreds of dollars and engaged expert workmen from Boston to make permanent repairs. The weathervane, a half ton in weight, was taken down and refurbished, cement coverings were spread over the upper platforms, and iron rods strengthened the resistance to wind. The vigilance of Sarah Potter has preserved the steeple from decay.

The bell is one to incite investigation for around its neck is the trade mark, "Boston Copper Company." This is not the name that was adopted by the "Revere Bell Foundry" after it is supposed that it ceased to cast bells. The tradition in Acworth has been constantly cherished that its bell was purchased from the Revere Company, as it doubtless was, although it is not listed in the Paul Revere records, neither are several other authentic specimens, found elsewhere in New Hampshire.

Unfortunately changes must affect meeting-houses, progress is advanced sometimes with regret. To conform to the necessities of a small village, the interior has been remodeled, the only exterior changes are colored glass windows in the upper auditorium. One should sympathize with the desire for a comfortable place of worship since Sabbath service was the intention of those who wrought with all their skill to build this beautiful structure in 1820.

On the Summit at Acworth

This front view of this masterpiece of colonial architecture possesses remarkable detail. Craftsmen carved the arches above the triple doors, and the frames of the Palladian windows. A scrutiny of its steeple on page one hundred thirty-six will excite admiration for the skilled artisans of a century ago.

THE DETAIL OF THE CORNICE
AT ACWORTH

This pattern of triangular corbels was originated by an unknown New England craftsman. The Ionic capital on the grooved pilasters is exquisitely executed.

The Bell in Acworth

THE REVERE BELL AT ACWORTH

Around the dome is the signature, Boston
Copper Company, which was used instead of Revere Copper Company in 1828 on a few bells.

The Meeting-house at Rindge
1797

STORIED STEEPLES

THE STEEPLE AT RINDGE

A third type of steeple distinguished by rectangular stories in contrast to octagons, is found in the border town of Rindge. Since this was one of the first towns to be granted to men who fought in the Indian Wars, Rindge does not lack for animated historical interest either in its secular affairs or ecclesiastical aspects.

Successive buildings housed the voters and the worshipers before the present edifice was erected in 1797. In the books of the town are found many quaint records, such as: "Any of the inhabitants shall have the liberty to work at cutting timbers for the meeting-house and to score in and but off for the huers for common wages, that is such hands as the committee shall think proper to employ." The significance of that last clause should not be overlooked. Sixteen town meetings opened and adjourned before the frame of the old meeting-house was sold for a barn, or John and Davis Barker received the contract for the new structure.

Again in the accounts of the town are expenses for workmen: for "vitualling—31 pounds; liquors and other stew—25 pounds; lemons and cider—one pound; sold rum barrel for 4s. 9d."

At the raising a committee of "deacons and Majors," the religious and military element, was chosen "to clear the ground of all idle spectators when they are in the way of the workmen."

After appointing a committee to "dignify the pews" meaning to decide which seats were the more honorable, "A grave responsibility and one requiring the exercise of great wisdom and prudence," once again the cautious voters, "fearing that these men would secure for themselves seats too exalted," chose a second committee, "To curb the self-esteem of the first." Did the town-fathers lack the finesse of present politicians?

A prominent resident of Rindge furnished the information that according to all the facts which she had been able to ascertain, the steeple was designed by a group of citizens either in a town meeting or an assembly called for the purpose. Once the spire was in better proportion to the size of the building. In after years a hand pump was pur-

145

chased for the fire-department by the town. Do their best, the fire-men were unable to force a stream of water above the weathervane. To accommodate the department, twelve feet were cut from the height of the spire, when the steeple was repaired.

Town records contain regulations about the length of the inter-mission between the morning and afternoon sermons on the Sabbath, the salary of the minister, and the exclusion of dogs "from the doors of the sanctuary."

Originally the pews faced the pulpit which was set against the west wall. In 1837, in accordance with a fad of modernists of that period, the pulpit was moved to the east wall between the doors from the vestibule and the seats were turned to face the east. The floor was graduated by flights of broad steps until the back pews were raised upon a platform nearly half way up the height of the west wall. The reason for this innovation was said to permit the congregation "to watch the brides enter church." Again in 1871 the pulpit was returned to its original position and the pews were rearranged to face the minister.

As in Hancock, the building is shared by town and Congregational Society, "Equal rights being voted to both town and Society to pass in and out of the front doors." The town also agreed "to keep the bell and its appendages in repair and build a new cupola above it when necessary."

To find an early prototype of this steeple, old Dedham, Massachu-setts must be explored where the church was built in 1781.

Another famous steeple with rectangular stories is the "Old North"* near Salem Street in Boston from whose windows was signaled with lanterns the message to Paul Revere of the line of march by the British soldiers on their way to Lexington and Concord, on April 17, 1775,

> "One if by land and two if by sea,
> And I, on the opposite shore will be
> Ready to ride and spread the alarm
> Through every Middlesex village and farm."

That steeple fell during a hurricane in 1808 and was rebuilt after the original design, by Charles Bulfinch. The Old North is the oldest church in Boston, erected in 1723. So, the citizens of Rindge were in historical company when they planned the rectangles of their steeple.*

* SEE PAGE 94

STORIED STEEPLES

The Revere bell in Rindge was replaced by another from a different foundry in 1856. The dentil detail in the cornices and the spirelets relieve the otherwise severe plainness of the exterior, the rows of front windows emphasize repeated alterations during the years, and the broad expanse of green around the building minimizes the size of the edifice which, in fact, is the largest structure of its kind in the state.

To the citizens of Rindge, this old landmark on the broad common is a monument of pride because of its historical background as well as its contribution to the religious life of Rindge.

PARK HILL, WESTMORELAND

Not exactly hidden by the hills yet half-concealed, in the vicinity of Keene and Chesterfield is the hamlet in Westmoreland, called Park Hill. Here on a south sloping hillside is an oval village green surrounded by spacious colonial homesteads shaded by elms in front and adorned with old fashioned gardens in the rear. On the summit the meeting-house broods over all. To the north extends for miles and miles up the Connecticut Valley an unobstructed prospect of New Hampshire and Vermont of which the villagers are so proud that they admonish visitors to climb to the steeple to view the landscape o'er. The road pitches immediately down an almost precipitious slope toward the north. To appreciate the situation of the meeting-house in its beginning in 1762 it is necessary to drive over this hill because then it can be understood why the settlers on Park Hill were willing to contribute over two thousand pounds—not dollars—a most exorbitant sum in Revolutionary times, to move the building from the northeast corner of the North Cemetery down in the valley, to the top of Park Hill.

The house was begun in 1762 but left unfinished, probably raised and boarded. Then bitter disputes raged between the Baptists and the Standing Order; each determined to move the structure to a location of its own choosing. Finally in 1779, the building was taken apart, loaded upon ox teams and headed south. Major Leonard Keep, the shrewd taverner who was interested in the hamlet on the hill, offered the teamsters a barrel of rum if they would unload near his tavern. He considered it good business to locate the meeting-house adjacent to his house of enter-

147

Park Hill, Westmoreland — 1762   #1824

tainment. The rum was enticing; the bribe was accepted. There they left the timbers on the spot where they stand today, facing the village green. In September, 1779, the first service was held within its walls after its removal.

That a porch was built over the east and the west doorways and that a wooden dove hung above the high sounding board above the pulpit is about all that is known concerning the appearance of the early edifice. Fastened to the center of the ceiling over the lighting fixture is a centerpiece which is believed to have been the top of the sounding board of the original pulpit. If this is true, judging from its formation, probably this is the dome of the bell that hung above a wineglass pulpit.

Fifty years later, in 1824, twenty feet were added to the front and the steeple and portico were completed. Both are unique in design. In the popular pattern books of Asher Benjamin were drawings for chimney pieces that, in miniature, resemble this portico. Either from the "Country Builder's Assistant" or the "Rudiments of Architecture" suggestions might have been derived since several plates illustrate the entablature of the Tuscan-Doric order and the lintels for doors.

The specimens of wood-carving in the beaded and twisted mouldings—like the ornamentation frequently seen on colonial furniture—in the lintel of the triple doorways and the ancient chain detail in the cornices can be seen in no other meeting-house in the state.

The low steeple, especially the dome top, is suitable for its exposed position on this wind-swept height. It can be discerned along the highways of Vermont and New Hampshire from many miles away. However, only near-by can the carved fans of the spandrels or the latticed balustrade or the graceful form of the urns be enjoyed or appreciated.

The entire setting of Park Hill village is one of the richest gems of the landscape of New Hampshire. The combination of natural scenery and architectural excellence have produced a picture unsurpassed in rural New England. Fortunately the residents who occupy the colonial homes, at least during the summer, are preserving the peaceful atmosphere untainted by commercial intrusion or any sign of all that mars the landscape in many localities. When in need of restful recreation a visit to Park Hill will lift the spirit above the disturbing elements of daily existence.

The Tuscan-Doric Portico

THE TUSCAN-DORIC PORTICO

In the pattern books of Asher Benjamin may
be found chimney pieces from which this portico
may have been copied. The pairs of columns are
spread widely apart as if supporting a mantle. The
olive branches carved around the oval window are
also found at Hancock and Acworth.

Detail of the front at Park Hill

DETAIL OF THE FRONT AT PARK HILL

Unusual motives in the detail of this New Hampshire meeting-house are:—the chain pattern in the cornices; the Greek triglyphs in the frieze; and the Tuscan capitals of the columns.

Detail of the Cornice at Park Hill

DETAIL OF THE CORNICE

No cornice in New Hampshire is composed with more originality. Not less than ten patterns of moulding are combined here above this triple doorway. The twist and the bead designs are unusual on exteriors.

The Village Common
Lyme — 1810

STORIED STEEPLES

THE MEETING-HOUSE AT LYME

Another storied steeple is seen many miles further north in Lyme. This unusually large meeting-house in a comparatively small village is explained by the history of the township. In the days of the provincial government which had its seat of power in Portsmouth, Governor Benning Wentworth claimed that Vermont, then called The New Hampshire Grants, was included within his jurisdiction. While often-times the rich meadow land was reserved for the king and Benning Wentworth, the higher lands on both sides of the Connecticut River were granted to a group of proprietors. This was the situation in Lyme. In consequence the meeting-house lot was located on the New Hampshire side and the settlers all came to the meeting-house in Lyme from both sides of the stream.

Little is known about the construction of the present building in 1810. When the explorers visited here, the members of the parish proudly pointed out the wide boards in the pews and other ancient relics, but had little to tell about the early history. Although every clew has been canvassed, no record of the name of the architect, or of the source of the design for this substantial, triple storied tower has been discovered. At first sight, the arches above the doors suggested pictures of eastern mosques. The pointed windows indicated Gothic motives. Certainly, originality is displayed in this northern village. No steeple in all New England resembled this structure in 1810.

Across the spacious village green stands the Alden Tavern, built and managed for many years by a descendant of the Pilgrim John and Priscilla and one of the oldest in the country to still open its doors to the public. Behind the church but separted from its lot by the state highway is the ancient cemetery where sleep the founders of this beautiful New England village.

The entire Connecticut Valley is filled with the creative art of country builders which increases the charm of its natural beauty. The names of Elias Carter and Joel Patrick should be more widely known and their contribution to colonial architecture more highly appreciated; likewise other towns should verify and honor the fame of their master-builders.

From a Print of St. John's with the Ancient Tombs and Table Stones
Portsmouth

This church was erected in 1806 at the period when the designs of Charles Bulfinch were dominant. Here the Vinegar Bible and the other gifts of Queen Caroline may be seen. The interior is decorated with tablets in memory of distinguished persons who lived in Portsmouth in Colonial Days.

CHAPTER X

THE ANGLICAN CHURCH IN THE COLONY

PORTSMOUTH

From the day, sometime before 1640, that Sir Richard Gibson, who was the "first parson" at Strawberry Bank, was expelled by the voters because "he was wholly addicted to the hierachy and discipline of England in exercising his ministerial functions," there is no record of any Anglican form of worship in the Colony within the following ninety years. After New Hampshire became a royal province the influence of the king was too powerful to permit the Puritans to exercise entire control of religious affairs in Portsmouth. Consequently, in 1732 a site on the rise of the hill near the river bank was given by Mr. Hope of London for Queen's Chapel, named in honor of Queen Caroline, wife of George II, and the cost of the building was paid by the English Society for Propagating the Gospel in Foreign Parts. The Queen demonstrated her pleasure by presenting the infant parish with a silver communion service, several prayer books, a Bible and two elaborately carved chairs upholstered in royal red damask. The Bible proved to be one of four, now priceless, "Vinegar Bibles." In 1717 a compositor in the office of the king's printer, John Basket of Oxford, set the heading for one page as "The Parable of the Vinegar" instead of the "Vineyard" and forty Bibles were bound before the mistake was discovered. Thirty-six Bibles were collected and burned in England; four apparently had already been shipped to the Colonies, one this gift from the Queen. Rev. Arthur Browne became the distinguished first rector of the parish.

On the day before Christmas, 1806 during a fire that raged along Bow Street, Queen's Chapel was among the buildings destroyed including its contents except one chair, the communion plate, a prayer book, the font and the Vinegar Bible which Alexander Ladd rescued at the imminent risk of his life. The parish immediately erected the church, Georgian in architecture, known as St. John's, the name given to the parish in articles of incorporation in 1791. The interior furnishings were imported from England, among them a wine-glass pulpit and square pews. St. John's possesses more relics of ecclesiastical value than any other parish in New Hampshire and this church is always included in a list of historical churches of America.

Most notable among many of the eventful days in Queen's Chapel was the visit of George Washington in 1789 accompanied by his secretary, Tobias Lear, a native son of Portsmouth whose birthplace is now among the houses that are preserved by patriotic societies in the city. Escorted by Governor Langdon, Theodore Atkinson and his secretary, Washington sat beneath the red plush draperies in the former Royal Governor's pew on Sabbath morning and occupied one of the Queen's chairs. In the confusion after the fire this chair was not distinguished by any mark. Soon a duplicate was ordered and today no one can tell which is the original and more ancient piece.

THE UNION CHURCH AT WEST CLAREMONT

In the parish at West Claremont a few families had purchased farms from the proprietors of the Claremont Grant about 1760. Being followers of the Episcopal faith, they appealed to the Society for the Propagation of the Gospel in Foreign Parts, to send a missionary to teach their children and Rev. Samuel Peters came in response to this call. The Union Church Parish was organized with Rev. Ranna Cossit as rector in 1771. Troublesome times soon came to the godly rector who was accused of Tory sympathies and was forbidden to leave town except to exercise his priestly office.

Governor John Wentworth furnished the plans for the church; he also promised the nails and the glass when needed. However, before that date arrived, the Governor had fled to Halifax. The Revolutionary War dragged out its dreary length and several years in addition before the little chapel was finished in 1789. Its frame is one of the best examples of the period. A story is related that during a service of

160

worship a storm of tornado proportions suddenly raged. The audience rushed in terror to the door where their exit was halted by a carpenter who had been one of those workmen who framed the structure. Standing in the doorway, he assured the frightened people that he knew no storm could destroy the building. Heeding his convincing words, all remained within its shelter in safety.

In 1801 the belfry was erected and twenty years later twenty-five feet were added for a chancel. Several remodelings have since been carried out, among them the removal of the gallery in 1875. Fortunately the square pews of varying sizes and spindle ornamentation have remained intact. Many relics of its historical past are found in different places in the building.

Interior at West Claremont

These pews vary in size and have seats on three sides. Note the stove pipe which extends the length of the room to utilize the heat from its radiation.

Union Church, West Claremont

Mount Ascutney from Belfry, West Claremont

The Timbers of the Roof
West Claremont

THE ATTIC AT WEST CLAREMONT

The king post truss is braced with three struts extending to the rafters or tie beams. Methods of pinning the timbers may be studied at the rafter and again at the post. Note the girths between the king posts.

CORNISH STREET AND TRINITY

Several miles down the valley lies Cornish
close beside the Connecticut River and overshadow-
ed by Mount Ascutney across the stream in Vermont. At the northern entrance to the long street
stands an aged chapel with an even more ancient
"God's Acre" for the church yard. Known as
Trinity, this chapel has preserved the Anglican
form of worship since 1793. Years ago a balcony
surrounded three sides of its interior; its slip pews
are old pine with panels twenty-one inches wide;
feathered clapboards and small paned windows
also testify to its ancient history. Cornish Street
is another landmark, shaded by overhanging elms
and lined by brick homesteads.

HOLDERNESS AND TRINITY

No spot in all New Hampshire can boast of more human interest than another Trinity Chapel in Holderness, the only Episcopal church to supplant the "Standing Order" in the Colony. Holderness was originally granted to a group of proprietors who failed to secure their charter and in 1765, under the friendly auspices of Governor Benning Wentworth, the Judge of the Admiralty Court of his Majesty at Portsmouth, Samuel Livermore, obtained the charter to a tract that now includes the towns of Holderness and Campton. At that period the Pemigewasset River flowed on the east side of the wide meadows in a meandering oxbow since cut off by the rapid stream. On the high bank, opposite the present railroad station in Plymouth, Judge Livermore erected a framed dwelling whose small cellar hole and wider foundations may be seen to this day. Being a far sighted prophet, the Judge realized the trend of revolt in the Colony and in 1774 he retired to this sylvan retreat where he busily developed his saw and grist mills and became the influential overlord of the region. He had already married the daughter of Rev. Arthur Browne, rector of Queen's Chapel, Portsmouth, a lady of poised manner who was capable of curbing her irascible husband. In 1769, Judge Livermore had been appointed the king's Attorney General. His estate far in the wilderness did not permit him to administer his official duties as Governor John Wentworth desired and the orders to present himself in Portsmouth or Wolfeboro could be easily set aside. Finally the Governor came to Holderness to be received by a judge of the king's court clothed in garments, borrowed from the miller, covered with dust from his grist mill; with an excuse—visibly displayed—that his business prevented him from leaving his estate. John Wentworth was too heartily in sympathy with the king's attorney to betray his advisor. The Governor sat on the curb of the cold spring down by the river's bank and drank toddy that had been chilled in the depths of the mountain waters while he discussed the state of the Colony until a servant announced dinner which was served in stately dignity by Mrs. Livermore.

THE ANGLICAN CHURCH IN THE COLONY

When the humble settlers of Holderness selected a site for their Puritan meeting-house, since called "Church Hill" and buried their dead in its adjacent town burial lot, Judge Livermore decreed otherwise. Years went by with no place for public worship in that section of the town. At length, Judge Livermore built the small chapel in 1797 which stands in Trinity church yard. The judge, his wife, and several of his off-spring lie beneath table tomb stones almost under the eaves. Holderness was Episcopalian.

With few changes in its interior, this small chapel remains intact with its slip pews in the center, the hinges of their doors creaking in protest of any movement. The square pews line the walls, that of the Judge and that of his son, Arthur, side by side, because the family trait of peppery dispositions descended from father to son and even in their religious devotions their quarrels separated them in different pews during Sabbath worship. Nevertheless, the Judge possessed a most generous nature. His deeds of mercy and kindness are still remembered. On one occasion when the house and barn of a settler was destroyed by fire in the autumn, Judge Livermore sent his teams loaded with provisions and fodder in sufficient quantity to sustain the unfortunate family and their cattle until spring. The pulpit of polished pine is as high as the ceiling permits and, strange to relate, its design is Puritan rather than wine-glass like those usually found in Anglican chancels.

The judge erected a mansion house which after his demise became the dormitory of Holderness School for Boys and in later years was burned. The Livermore family has scattered far and wide and only the locust trees and the wild roses of the garden that surrounded the first homestead remain to perpetuate the memory of the founder of Trinity in Holderness.

On page one hundred seventy nine is a picture of the first Catholic Chapel in New Hampshire. In 1818, the rector of the Union Church decided to return to his former allegiance to the Catholic faith, and his son followed him. In 1823, the brick chapel was completed in the cemetery lot, opposite the Union Church at West Claremont. The lower room was consecrated to services of worship; the upper story was a school for boys which flourished another forty years.

TRINITY IN HOLDERNESS

This diminutive chapel is the only Anglican
Church which was the meeting-house of the town
in New Hampshire. Beneath the eaves are the
table stones above the graves of the Livermore
Family.

THE PULPIT AT TRINITY

Although Judge Livermore was Episcopal in
his form of worship, he placed a Puritan design
instead of wine-glass for the pulpit in his chancel.
Slip pews had become popular in 1797, but square
stalls are around the walls.

Quaker Meeting-house in Dover
1760

CHAPTER XI

QUAKERS IN NEW HAMPSHIRE

Quakers first appeared in the Massachusetts Bay Colony in Boston in 1656 to the alarm of the magistrates. Stringent laws were passed to banish them. Finally three were hanged on Boston Common in punishment for repeated returns from their exile.

Four of the hated sect came to Dover in 1662 and, to the distress of "Priest Rayner," the people listened to their preaching about the mysterious "inner light" that sustained them in adversity.

Richard Waldron, chief townsman, ordered that three Quaker women be stripped to the waist, tied to the cart's tail and whipped out of the colony with not over ten stripes each. This order was executed in Dover, then the women were carried on horseback to Hampton where the same torture was inflicted, and again in Salisbury. In the next town, the magistrate refused to obey the instruction but sent the women to the home of Major Shapleigh in Kittery, Maine, who harbored them until their wounds had healed. Then the Quakers returned to Dover to preach their faith. This so angered the magistrates that the women were dragged through the snow to the Piscataqua River and placed in a canoe to transport them again to Major Shapleigh, a man who feared no magistrate or the doctrine of the Quakers. A tempest arose, upset the canoe, tossed the Quakers into the river. However, they clung to the canoe and were dragged back to the land where they were confined in the unheated prison. At mid-night, the magistrates determined to banish these dissenters from Dover. Again they were placed in a boat, although their clothing was still frozen, and they were returned to Kittery. Regardless of the exposure, the Quakers survived and in time returned to Dover. Finally the magistrates permitted the sect to live in the town in peace and allowed them to build a chapel in 1680.

Today in the southern part of the city stands a Quaker meeting-house that was erected in 1760, surrounded by the cemetery. Like all of their houses of worship, the auditorium may be divided into two rooms when the sexes wish to hold separate services. A partition extends through the center about three feet in height and above this hangs, on hinges from the ceiling, a paneled screen that can be raised or lowered as desired. A separate doorway is always found among the Quakers for the men and for the women.

Prosperity blessed these righteous citizens of Dover. Their colonial homes line the street near their meeting-house where their descendants live to this day.

The Quaker Meeting-house near Acworth
1820

QUAKERS IN NEW HAMPSHIRE

Gradually the Quakers penetrated to the interior of the state. Their chapels are found in Henniker, Weare and Acworth. At Weare several groups settled in separate villages and a Quaker academy was established in 1834, with Moses Austin Cartland of Lee, its first principal. One of the buildings is now used as the public schoolhouse and on the playground is a tablet to mark the site of the first building of Clinton Grove Academy. Across the street another bronze marker preserves the ground of an early meeting-house and its ancient "Upping Stone."

On a remote country by-way near Acworth may be found a weather-beaten, one story chapel built by the Quakers of "Quaker City" in 1820. Under the locust trees are the graves of many who worshiped here a century ago. No descendants are now living in the vicinity but once a year the Quakers gather from other towns to hold a service in the little chapel. The hanging screen is paneled old pine, the work of skilled craftsmen; the benches are rude and uncomfortable, and the unpainted clapboards will soon fall to decay.

The Quakers were excellent citizens although they refused to pay tithes, to take off their hats to the magistrates, or to travel on the Sabbath. Their aversion to war was respected even in the days of the Revolution. A story is recalled in Henniker, however, which proves that a Quaker could adjust his religion to the necessity of his country if called to duty in an emergency. Quaker Brown settled in Hopkinton before the beginning of the Revolutionary War. After the Battle of Bunker Hill a courier rode into the town with a message to summons men to assist in driving the British out of Boston. The smartest man and the fleetest horse were demanded to carry this news to Warner and Sutton. Mathew Stanley was selected as the man to carry the message and Quaker Brown was said to possess the fleetest mare. When Mr. Stanley requested the use of the animal, Quaker Brown replied, "Thou knowest, Friend Stanley, that I am a man of peace and cannot allow my mare to be used for any such purpose." Stanley replied, "By the Powers, I will have her!" Then said Quaker Brown, "Very well; since thou wilt have her, she is in yonder pasture and the saddle and bridle hang in the mill-house." The mare was caught by Stanley, and rode to his errand. On his return he replaced the saddle and bridle where he found them and turned the mare into the pasture with no further remonstrance from the man of peace.

Isles of Shoals
1800

QUAKERS IN NEW HAMPSHIRE

THE ISLES OF SHOALS

Before the mainland of New Hampshire was settled by white men, the English fishermen used the Isles of Shoals for a summer colony about 1575. Captain John Smith gave the isles his name in 1614. Later a fishing village of six hundred souls was called Gossport, on Star Island. Several meeting-houses were built, only to be burned by ungodly fishermen, according to tradition.

Then in 1800 a stone chapel was erected with its interior furnishings manufactured from the timbers of a Spanish wreck. The village has disappeared; except for the grass-grown cemetery, all traces of the former settlers are lost. Many monuments mark historic sites, memorials of those who once lived on the islands while above them all the little stone chapel guards the graves of a forgotten people.

First Catholic Chapel in New Hampshire
West Claremont — 1820

179

Meeting-house at Canterbury

THE SHAKERS

Another sect which has preserved a meeting-house of 1792 are the Shakers of Canterbury. These followers of Ann Lee established two prosperous colonies in New Hampshire; one at Enfield, the other in Canterbury, during the eighteenth century. The latter occupies an extensive estate where their high-bred cattle and richly fertilized acres have long been famous. Few of their sect remain while the Enfield colony has now disappeared completely. Disbelieving in marriage and living a communistic existence, they observed a form of religious worship which included a peculiar dance from which their name was derived. Their gambreled roofed meeting-house of 1792 may be visited where a Shaker Sister in her quaint costume will display the arts which are still practiced among the few men and women who occupy the spacious dwellings that once housed several hundred followers.

180

CHAPTER XII

BEYOND NEW HAMPSHIRE

Curiosity prompted several explorations to learn about the meeting-houses that were preserved in other states. Since concentration upon a hobby and elimination of all distractions intensifies vision to a remarkable degree, our eyes were on steeples, wherever we strayed.

CONNECTICUT

One April morning a motor was packed with equipment for a trip into southern New England with the intention of a zig-zaging course just to collect pictures and data to supplement colonial New Hampshire. April was the ideal month for antiquarians to tour. The trees had no summer verdure that concealed old houses with their ornamental cornices and overhangs. The sleepy towns were still enjoying the peace of winter vacation from tourists and traffic. They were natural, devoid of haste, at leisure to reply to inquisitive visitors.

How we admired the wide streets of those Connecticut towns along the coastal plain. They seemed to echo the voices of their ancient planning boards, declaring, "Here is land a plenty and to spare for spacious beauty." No narrow valleys and boulder strewn hill-sides hemmed them in as in New Hampshire. They could be as lavish as they pleased with their pine forested floor. Today, as beneficiaries of their generosity, Connecticut has an heritage of enviable landscaping. Elms in double phalanx stretch many, many miles along its highways. Hundreds of seventeenth and eighteenth century houses, once the center of wide-spreading farms, now sophisticated patriarchs, surround village greens or border park-like streets. How grateful we were for those dignified date-plates that were fastened, proudly no doubt, to the house-walls, so clearly lettered that he who rode might read. We found overhangs on gable

181

ends at both attic and second floor levels, Georgian doorways and gambreled roofs, old stone houses and wishing wells. But we were seeking meeting-houses and steeples. When we were back in our homes, the pictures were spread out for comparison. Four eighteenth century meeting-houses were found in Connecticut: Brooklyn, Farmington, Wethersfield and East Haven. Two Puritan steeple designs were discovered at Washington. The ability of Ithiel Towne was demonstrated at New Haven on the Green, with his Gibbs pattern for the steeple.

A Puritan Steeple at Washington

BROOKLYN

Brooklyn, 1771, and Amherst, New Hampshire, were identical, their steeples designed from the same pattern book, without doubt. A tablet attached to the outside wall was dedicated to the hero, Colonel Israel Putnam, a native of the town, under whose leadership this meeting-house was erected. After the Colonel had made his name famous for his deeds of valor in the Revolution, he received the honor at home of being elected caretaker of the meeting-house and bell ringer at a salary of three pounds a year and when he died in 1790 he was again honored with the unusual distinction of a funeral in the meeting-house, not a common custom in those days.

FARMINGTON

Farmington, 1770, retained its religious aspect. Although its interior had been modernized somewhat, it is still the village church. Its steeple, mentioned in another chapter, resembles the Old South except that its spire is far more slender, like a tapering needle surmounted by a weathervane. Somewhat gruesome to think about was the ancient whipping-post which is utilized today as the foundation for the church bulletin board, a most appropriate successor to that instrument of punishment for public exhibition before the south doors of the meeting-house.

The East Doorway at Farmington

WETHERSFIELD

Wethersfield is a beautiful brick meeting-house of 1761, first of its material in the state, manufactured of Connecticut's clay and laid in Flemish bond. Onions were the medium of barter for these farmers in Connecticut to pay for their meeting-house taxes.

An ascent to the attic revealed the same king-post and double rafter framework of that period which was the custom everywhere. In the upper corridor the parapet of the high pulpit is preserved. It has festoons of hand carved roses, resembling the wreaths that Grinling Gibbons carved for Sir Christopher Wren in St. Paul's cathedral in London in 1697.

The Parapet of the Colonial Pulpit

The base resembles a shell and its surface is weathered to the soft brown of old growth pine. The custodian displayed an ancient batten door and the plate of an early communion service. Otherwise the modifications had removed all traces of age from the interior and the atmosphere of two centuries could not be imagined as in buildings that are constructed from wooden timbers.

The elaborate geometric design laid in the brick courses on the front of the square tower distinguishes the building throughout New England; also the steeple, with rectangular stories resembles the minsters of old England. More ancient are the stones above the graves of the founders of Wethersfield in the rear of the church, bearing the names of families from whom the explorers proudly traced their descent.

BEYOND NEW HAMPSHIRE

EAST HAVEN

In East Haven is a stone building of 1774 with a steeple of a much later date and its interior entirely transformed from any colonial appearance. No old square pews or high pulpits were found in Connecticut.

Two periods of later architecture predominated, the Georgian of Asher Benjamin and the Greek Revival of 1830. The portico, usually in the Ionic order, was universally seen and the steeple, consisting of two octagonal lanterns and spire, like the Asher Benjamin plates, was

Georgian Architecture at Avon — 1820

found at Avon, Guilford, Milford "new lights," Cheshire, South Britain and Litchfield, with Milford "old lights," and Branford almost identical designs.

The Greek Revival with its porch of the Doric order and square tower and belfry was found at Colchester, Saybrook, Clinton, Middlebury, Southington, Norwichtown, Windsor and Simsbury—all indicating the influence of the period of 1830.

All of these churches were built within thirty years, from 1810-1840, all were modern types with the influence of Bulfinch displayed either in their porticoes or their doorways.

Greek Revival at Windsor — 1830

Springfield

MASSACHUSETTS STRUCTURES

As we rode northward through the Connecticut Valley in Massachusetts, at Longmeadow and Springfield the ancient village green and the meeting-house are preserved as of long ago. Regardless of crowded streets in the midst of its financial district, Springfield has retained its central open space with the church and city hall occupying lots around it.

The surrounding towns have many churches of colonial architecture. At Hadley are several gems of New England art. Few buildings retain their meeting-house appearance.

189

BEYOND NEW HAMPSHIRE

ROCKY HILL IN SALISBURY, MASSACHUSETTS

Danville, Sandown and Fremont have a rival across the state line in Salisbury, Massachusetts. Doubtless this is the masterpiece of early colonial meeting-houses in New England, situated on the brow of Rocky Hill, not far from Amesbury, Massachusetts. On August 1st, 1785, the town voted after six months of wrangling, to "build on the eastward side of the parsonage house." The construction was so far advanced by December that a town meeting convened beneath its roof. Possibly the expedition was due to two skilled housewrights, Timothy Palmer of Newburyport and Jacob Spofford of Bradford, Massachusetts. Seven years later, 1792, Timothy Palmer became famous as the engineer who bridged the Merrimack River from Salisbury to Newbury and again in 1794 over the Piscataqua from Portsmouth to Kittery. In partnership with Jacob Spofford, their firm built bridges over the Susquehanna River, the Schuykill at Philadelphia and the Potomac at Washington. To Timothy Palmer is credited the idea of a roof above his wooden arches which became the New England covered bridge. Because of the accurate mathematical principles in his arches and the mechanical stability of his bridges, Timothy Palmer was known as the most eminent engineer in New England at his period.

In volume thirty-six of the Granite Monthly Magazine may be seen a picture of this meeting-house with the statement that Rocky Hill was an exact copy of another which was erected at Hampton Falls, New Hampshire in 1760. The porch over the south doorway is unusual with a stairway to the gallery on this one side only. In the long walls many windows were possible, a natural heating plant and only source of warmth provided by twelve hundred panes of glass to attract the sun's rays.

Doubtless the high pulpit was the design most often found in New England, sometimes called the tulip pulpit, deriving this name because the projection beneath the desk resembled the corolla of that flower. A labyrinth of narrow aisles divided the stall pews into so many shapes and sizes that one is curious to learn by what method these seats were "dignified" by the seating committee. Did the size of a family, or the

191

The Base of the Tulip Pulpit

price the owner paid or his position in the town, perhaps all three, determine who should occupy the conspicuous front sections?

A citizen of Salisbury wrote as follows: "Rocky Hill is a rich legacy. Erected one hundred forty-eight years ago and today in just as good condition with no changes since it was built. Its story ties us up to the great "Father of His Country," George Washington. When he made his famous tour of this section of the country in 1789, the first year he was President, he stopped overnight at Newburyport. The next morning he crossed the Merrimac River at the "Ferry" in Amesbury, landing on Merrimac Street and then rode on horse-back along the point shore and up the Rocky Hill Road to the meeting-house. Two companies, the Amesbury and Salisbury Militia, were drawn up on the plain near the building. Standing on the steps of the meeting-house, he addressed the soldiers. When we realize that this ancient building is preserved to us just as it looked when Washington visited it on that memorable day, so long ago, its worth can be more fully appreciated.

"The services that are held there each summer are of more than ordinary interest and naturally attract many of the tourists who are in this section of the country."

Fortunately the building has been in the custody of a devoted neighboring family who have cherished its history and guarded its entire body from the ravages of time. Basking in the sunshine, protected by the brow of the hill, on its well drained site, there is every reason to expect several centuries will pass before its timbers fall to dust.

The Choir Stall in the Front Gallery
with its rail on the Parapet

193

The Tulip Base at Plymouth, New Hampshire

When the meeting-house at Plymouth was sold for a barn, a devout woman salvaged the high pulpit. Her husband did not reverence its pine panels and cut the greater part for kindling wood. Only two panels and this base of the pulpit were snatched from the ax. This relic was stored in the bell loft of the new church, 1836, and entirely forgotten during many years. It now serves in the chancel as a lectern and one of the panels is inserted in the front parapet of the recent pulpit. There is no doubt that tulip pulpits were the more usual design throughout the state, in colonial meeting-houses.

The High Pulpit at Rocky Hill, Salisbury — 1789

The Meeting-house at Sheffield
about 1785

BEYOND NEW HAMPSHIRE

SHEFFIELD, MASSACHUSETTS

Another summer trip found us in the Housatonic Valley in Sheffield, Massachusetts dining at the Inn. The scribe hastily finished her dessert and requested to be excused. Immediately the chauffeur reminded her that there were miles to go before we slept and remarked, "I tried to call your attention to the other side of the street with a hope that you did not notice that old church." Smilingly, came the reply, "My Dear, I have known for years that that old church was here and have been guiding the route this way all the morning that I might see it." Resigned, the good man said, "Don't keep us too long!" Hurrying down the street, there seemed to be only time to ask the first person who appeared for information about the age of the fine old building. "Well, I don't know," was the reply, "but here comes Miss——— and I think she can tell you." A spinster, indeed, approached who did look promising. However, she gazed at the visitor with New England reticence and said that she could not tell when the church was built. After some words of praise had aroused her pride in the town's possession of the building although she evidently was not one of its sect, she gave the Asher Benjamin steeple an appraising glance, admitted that it was beautiful and then came just the story desired, "It was built long ago, perhaps a hundred and fifty years and was moved here from the hill." "Two stories?" "No, the interior was as it was then built with galleries on three sides." Satisfied we motored on our way.

VERMONT

Before we left that side of the Berkshires, we visited old Bennington where another Asher Benjamin steeple is famous—built in 1806—a copy of plate 33 in the "Country Builder's Assistant" as illustrated on the following page. There is the design for Ashby and Washington steeples, there is also the plan of a Bulfinch pulpit proving that Mr. Benjamin printed the patterns of contemporary architects of his day.

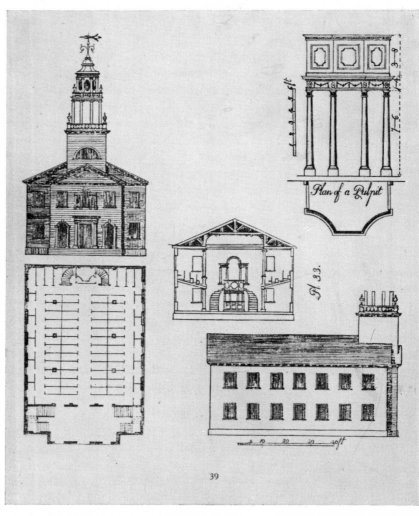

Plan of a Pulpit

39

Plate 33 from Asher Benjamin's Country Builder's Assistant, displaying a plan for a meeting-house

ROCKINGHAM — 1789

Autumn was the season to visit Rockingham, Vermont, on its sightly knoll, just off the beaten track, among the red maples.

It was built in 1787 by a committee appointed by the state legislature although the town of Rockingham in 1774 had voted that "the trustees find four Gallons of Rum to raise and frame said house." The master-builder, Gen. Ebenezer or John Fuller—both names are found—quietly took his place on the beam at the raising and "went up" with the front, broadside, says Hayes' History of Rockingham, "although his weight was two hundred fifty pounds." The key was put up at auction to the lowest bidder who gave bonds that he would unlock the door every

Sunday morning and lock it at evening and at all other public meetings at all times, with a penalty attached of four cents for each neglect of duty. He also agreed to sweep the house four times a year, during the first week of every three months with a forfeit of fifty cents for each neglect. Nevertheless, there was a local idea that to be permitted to guard this key was an "honor."

After 1832, only town meetings convened here; the structure was sadly neglected. Restoration was accomplished in 1906, for the most part through the influence of Miss Elizabeth Thompson. The beauty of the south doorway merits an illustration.

The South Doorway

200

BEYOND NEW HAMPSHIRE

At Windsor the Congregational church retains its meeting-house exterior, erected in 1797, and an Asher Benjamin steeple stands above the porch, probably an addition in the early years of the nineteenth century.

An unusually ornate lantern of a Puritan belfry is at Strafford. Also, the bell-top of the sounding board is preserved.

ANCIENT MEETING-HOUSES IN MAINE

Several colonial meeting-houses are standing today in Maine in the vicinity of Wiscasset, relics of the workmanship of ship's carpenters. The oldest is at Walpole, 1772; two at Alna, 1789; and a German edifice at Waldoboro, 1794, which contains a collection of German Bibles and communion plate of ancient design.

THE MEETING-HOUSE AT ALNA

Turning inland at Wiscasset, a hilly road ascends to a wind-swept hill-top where a meeting-house of 1789 is situated. A tablet on the front states the age of the edifice and the fact that it has been restored by the Pemiquid Chapter of the D. A. R. The north and south walls are covered by "ship-lapped" clapboards; the east and west ends by narrow hand made shingles and so this has always been from its beginning. One door, only, enters a vestibule that contains the stairway to the gallery, as at Rocky Hill.

Again a friendly custodian, Mr. Clarence Walker, proudly unlocked the ancient door and told the story of the building. Several years ago the interior was restored to its original appearance. Every spindle was in place in the frames around all the pews; the pew doors hung on their original hinges and the wrought iron scrapers remain on the doorstones. The pulpit which resembles the design at Walpole, has the most ornamental stairway of any we have discovered.

The old town records state that Joseph Carleton was the master-builder and Mr. Walker has been told that his ancestors were also among the workmen who turned the spindles. Mr. Carleton had some original ideas about framing as his trusses indicate. Six king-posts support the roof, each braced with struts that extend to the double rafters

The Pulpit at Alna, Maine — 1789

but, only between the two central trusses are cross timbers braced length-wise of the frame; three crosses being the usual number elsewhere. This meeting-house possessed more than an architectural charm to the explorers, because of the fact that in 1796 Rev. Jonathan Ward was ordained as minister in Alna. Jonathan was the youngest son of Parson Nathan Ward, first minister in Plymouth, New Hampshire in 1765. Like his father, Jonathan was a man of pronounced convictions. His aversion to the bass viol in the sanctuary prevented its introduction in Alna's choir for many years. At length the preacher was outvoted. Then he yielded to modern trends by announcing to his congregation on the first Sunday after the hated instrument appeared, that they would sing the one hundred nineteenth psalm and "fiddle it to their hearts content." Since the metrical version of this Song of David fills many pages of the old "Psalter," the sense of humor which saves many difficult situations, was praiseworthy in Parson Jonathan Ward.

In another section of Alna, a second meeting-house remains but its structure has not been preserved intact to the same degree as this 1789 edifice.

THE MEETING-HOUSE AT WALPOLE

After repeated inquiries and miles of desultory driving we discovered the quaint meeting-house in Walpole, Maine, standing on a knoll beside a grass-grown roadway behind a thicket of birches that conceal it from the highway that ends at Christmas Cove. On the door was a placard giving directions to several custodians of the keys to the building. Re-tracing many miles of crisscross roads, we found Mr. George A. Huston who courteously acted as our guide. He explained how vandals had compelled the church committee to establish an ironclad rule that no visitors be allowed in the building unless accompanied by a member of the church committee. After we had admired the antique fixtures about the pulpit and noted the absence of others, the sad fact was deplored that theft is practiced even in an ancient sanctuary.

It is not surprising that this structure is not easily found. No white clapboards make it conspicuous. Instead, the exterior is covered by rough, hand-split shingles that, once upon a time, were either painted or stained a brownish yellow that so resembles the autumn color of the birch leaves as to camouflage it among the trees. In size and shape, Walpole resembles its contemporary, Sandown; even the arrangement of the pews on the lower floor is identical also. Here, however, is a more completely finished interior. The rough posts of the frame are concealed by planed casements with beveled corners; the woodwork is painted a dull grey color; the windows are furnished with twenty-four of the smallest panes of old glass that we have seen.

The pulpit is a masterpiece by skilled ship-carpenters and unlike any design elsewhere. If the tulip base designates the pattern of Rocky Hill, then the daisy must have been the inspiration for this one in Walpole. A mottled green paint, to simulate Italian marble, covers both the pulpit and the posts that support the gallery. One of the most curious relics we have found is the hinge to the door that enters the pulpit pew. A double jointed semi-circular section permits the door to slip by into the pulpit enclosure a few inches so, as it swings, it does not obstruct the narrow landing at the top of the stairway.

Again, a reversed plan for the pews was found in the gallery. On its floor the square pews lined the parapet while the usual long slip pews were built on raised step-like platforms behind the family pews. Balancing upon the railing of the rear pew, we were able to lift our heads through the cubbyhole in the ceiling to study the framework of the roof. To our surprise, the timbers were about half the size of other structures of this period and queen-post trusses with single rafters supported the roof. As in Sandown, the wedged or "locked" joints held the struts firmly in position.

As we returned with Mr. Huston to his home, he indicated the site of the first log cabin of his ancestors which they rolled up three hundred years ago. In fear of the hostile Kennebec Indians, the family fortunately abandoned this home as winter approached. When they returned in the spring, only the ashes of the logs remained. In his small workshop, Mr. Huston has collected a remarkable legacy of ancient tools from his grandfathers through several generations. Here are circular "T" augers for boring holes in huge timbers to receive the long wooden pins or trun'ls as they were called in the vernacular of ship carpenters. A most valuable exhibit was a complete set of thirty or more small hand planes that were used to carve mouldings and panels of many designs.

The Pulpit at Walpole

COLONIAL MEETING-HOUSES IN NEW HAMPSHIRE

Mr. Huston advised us to watch along the highway in Woolwich near Nequasset Pond for a small meeting-house which is the oldest in the vicinity, perhaps in Maine dating from 1762. Although the building is now transformed from its ancient appearance, we found the little structure in an ancient cemetery not far from the highway.

THE GERMAN MEETING-HOUSE AT WALDOBORO

The town of Waldoboro, Maine, was settled in 1748 by emigrants from Germany. In its ancient cemetery are three monuments. One commemorates Conrad Heyer, born April 10, 1749, first child born of European parents in Waldoboro. He died in 1856 at the age of one hundred six years. The other two stones were erected to the memory of two pastors: Rev. Frederick Augustus Rodolphus Ritz, born in Germany in 1752, and Rev. John Wm. Starman, born in Germany in 1773.

Waldoboro, Maine
1772 — 1797

BEYOND NEW HAMPSHIRE

A log meeting-house was dedicated in 1763. Soon this building became too small for the increasing population and sometime before 1773 a framed house was erected which remained unfinished without doors or windows while benches were the only seats.

The inhabitants feared to leave their homes to attend religious services until the war between France and England was finished. After the treaty of peace was signed, Rev. John Shaffer preached to a crowded house from the one hundred thirty-seventh Psalm in the German language. The history of Waldoboro states that these people who had worshiped in gorgeous churches, rejoiced that after so many years they could assemble in a rude meeting-house and worship the same God under the same form of religion as they had been privileged in Germany.

For a generation the building stood on the east bank of the Medomak River and some of the worshipers were obliged to ferry across the stream to attend services. In 1795 the building was moved across the river to its present site. Its dimensions are thirty-six feet by forty-five and the posts are twenty feet high. The original sills were twelve by thirteen inches in size. Cross timbers of the same size are still in use, part of white pine and others of black ash. A large porch containing several doorways covers the one entrance to the auditorium. A gallery runs around the sides of the interior and unpainted square pews with seats around three of their sides furnish the sittings. The pulpit and parapet of the gallery were once painted. The pulpit desk is nine feet above the floor but no pew for the deacons stands below it. Probably this form of church organization was not practiced among the Germans. A quaint home-made communion table and contribution boxes are preserved. As was often the custom, an ancient stove has its funnel passing through a window since the building has no chimney.

In a cabinet are exhibited the original communion service and a collection of books including many old Bibles, printed in German.

Around the building is an ancient God's Acre which is known today as the German Protestant Cemetery of Waldoboro. Once a summer a service of worship is held in the ancient edifice, an event in the town.

Few emigrants from Germany settled in New England and this is the only sanctuary of its faith in this part of the country that the explorers have discovered.

COLONIAL MEETING-HOUSES IN NEW HAMPSHIRE

SANCTUARIES OF RHODE ISLAND

Although we found no meeting-houses in the strict definition of the term, in Rhode Island, this historic state has many shrines that should be visited in an ecclesiastical tour of New England. A native daughter of Rhode Island proudly accompanied us on an exploration of her state.

No spot is more crowded with buildings of historical significance than in the vicinity of Touro Street in Newport. Here is the lot that was purchased by Dutch Jews in 1677 and used to the present day by the Hebrews as a burial ground. Close by is the Jewish Synagogue that was designed by Peter Harrison, famous architect who came to this country with Bishop Berkley in 1728. The building was erected in 1759-63 and is the oldest belonging to the Hebrews in the country. George Washington sat beside the Jewish elder here on his visit to Newport in 1789. Twelve Corinthian pillars support the ceiling, emblematic of the twelve tribes of Israel.

Perhaps the Seventh Day Baptist Church may be called a meeting-house as it was erected in 1729. It is now the property of the Newport Historical Society which regards it with such reverence that the walls are encased with brick with iron shutters over the windows. The roof decayed and a slate cover protects the ancient trusses. The panels of the old pews and walls are preserved in the wainscoting. The high pulpit, the original clock and the Tables of the Law are attached to the walls as of old.

Around the corner on Church Street stands old Trinity, built in 1726 and surrounded by the graves in the ancient church yard. In appearance the building is the New England meeting-house type with its two tiers of windows and its storied steeple. Within, the wine-glass pulpit is placed on the east side, as was the custom of the Church of England, in the center of the chancel. Although it has been refitted with modern pipes, the case of the organ which was given by Bishop Berkley is still in use. This gift was presented because the citizens honored the clergyman by assembling at the wharf when his ship landed from England in 1729

Near Wickford is St. Paul's Episcopal Chapel. It was first erected several miles from its present site in 1707 and was known as the Narragansett Church.

While the First Baptist Church in Providence is one of the finest examples of colonial architecture in New England it was never a meeting-house. This was constructed in 1771 to provide an auditorium of sufficient capacity to accommodate the commencement at Brown University. The steeple is copied from the pattern book by James Gibbs.

The Bulfinch Church at Lancaster, Massachusetts
1816

At Newbury — 1821

CHAPTER XIII

THE INFLUENCE OF CHARLES BULFINCH IN NEW HAMPSHIRE

As stated in a previous chapter, the transformation from the plan of the ancient meeting-house to the modern church was introduced by Charles Bulfinch at Pittsfield, Massachusetts in 1793. This radical modification appeared in New Hampshire at Fitzwilliam in 1816 although many other characteristics that distinguish the designs of Bulfinch were not incorporated in the churches of the state before 1821. In the following five years, three wooden structures were erected in widely separated communities that prove that the influence of this architect was rapidly penetrating into the Granite State.

NEWBURY

In Newbury, near Lake Sunapee, a small church, built in 1821, repays a visit in overflowing measure. Its exterior bears conclusive evidence that the master-builder was familiar with the work of Bulfinch. A wide porch across the front is entered through two arched doorways ornamented by fan-blinds in their pediments. Fan-shaped blinds above the windows and a belfry crowned by a dish-cover dome seem to establish the fact that the source of their designs was Charles Bulfinch. Above the wooden ball on the dome rises one of the most artistic weathervanes of wrought iron to be seen throughout the country-side, doubtless the production of a skilled local blacksmith. The interior presents peculiar interest. As the visitor enters the vestibule, the delicate tint of the green painted walls reminds one of the colonial custom that decorated interiors with this hint of apple green. Through the doorway, the arrangement of the slip pews is at first bewildering for they face the vestibule. Here is the one interior in the state which is now so seated although in East Derry is a semi-example of this century old custom. Bright red damask cushions contrast with the white painted pews and red carpets follow the color scheme.

The pulpit immediately absorbs the attention. It stands between the doors with a staircase ascending on either side to its platform. The semi-circular front is ornamented by delicate patterns of hand carving and four slender pillars support the platform as a substitute for the deacons' pew of the high colonial pulpits. If the student of Bulfinch's architecture will visit Lancaster, Massachusetts, a pulpit of elaborate design may be seen there in the Congregational church which is said to possess the greatest merit of all that Bulfinch planned in New England.

A Bulfinch Pulpit at Lancaster, Mass.

212

A Bulfinch Design at Newbury

COLONIAL MEETING-HOUSES IN NEW HAMPSHIRE

A number of years ago the trend of modernization influenced the villagers of Newbury to desire to remodel this interior to conform to up-to-date custom. Fortunately at that time Secretary and Mrs. John Hay, of international fame and recognition, were summer residents at Lake Sunapee. The appeals of this cultured couple were heeded and through their generous financial assistance, the restoration of the interior was carefully completed without despoiling the original plans. Because of this praiseworthy appreciation by Mr. and Mrs. Hay, the value of this unique little House of God was impressed upon the entire community. Today a custodian of the keys will graciously accompany visitors within its doors and explain the details of its history with pride in her voice. May Father Time be kind to this sacred edifice! Long may the little church at Newbury remain unchanged. Here is a museum piece of the 1820 decade.

The Meeting-house at the foot of the South Side
of Corser Hill in Webster and the Burying Ground

1789

THE INFLUENCE OF CHARLES BULFINCH

CORSER HILL IN WEBSTER

On the southern slope of Corser Hill in Webster is a town-house of 1789 which was deserted in 1823 on the Sabbath when the new church was dedicated on the top of the hill. Were it not for the unusual beauty of the fan-lights above the doors and windows, the exterior of the new edifice might seem uninteresting. On the contrary, the sash of the windows forms artistic patterns which are set with the clearest, sparkling panes of old glass that we found in all of our travels. When we were informed that the glass shades on the kerosene lamps, now electrified, were rare Sandwich patterns, then the age and origin of the window panes was suspected. Glass globes of frosted designs cover the lamps in the chandelier. One was then missing. The price of one hundred fifty dollars for a duplicate was a staggering sum to the sexton who accompanied us in our exploration. Fortunately since that day, a daughter of the town was delighted to discover a globe that so nearly matches its companions that its differences are unnoticed by the casual worshipers in the summer services that are always observed throughout the months when no heating plant is required.

The interior possesses a quaint charm. The rosy sheen of the surface of the San Domingo mahogany veneer on the century old pulpit, a design resembling Newington, displays a wealth of unusual beauty. Although slip pews were permitted to occupy the center of the auditorium, the fathers of Webster were not inclined to accept the new notions entirely. Consequently, they built square pews around the walls beneath the balcony. Within them is a relic of former customs—the notebook rests. These are inch thick boards about six inches wide and eighteen inches long that are fastened by hinges to small blocks of wood that are nailed to the wall resembling, in miniature, the ironing boards that hang in modern kitchens. If a listener wished to record the points of the sermon, he raised this shelf, braced it to position with a piece of wood provided for this purpose which fitted into another block below on the wall. Thus with his writing materials conveniently placed, he copied the sermon as desired. It was a bit of country gossip that the more illiterate the occupant of the pew, the more copious notes he appeared to write, to convince his neighbors of his ability with his quill.

At the Top of Corser Hill in Webster

The View from the Belfry on Corser Hill

Over the expanse of the Blackwater Valley, Mount Kearsarge and Mount Ragged dominate the horizon. In the foreground the roof of a colonial homestead surrounded by numerous barns differs from the other belfry views among the illustrations, because this belfry was erected after towns had ceased to build meeting-houses and church organizations chose sites for their new structures that were removed from the ancient burying grounds.

The Vestibule at Corser Hill

VESTIBULE AT CORSER HILL

The usual method of securing the doors is displayed in this bar that drops into staples or hooks on the jambs.

Sandwich glass shades ornament the lamps and sparkling panes fill the sashes.

Wentworth
1825

THE INFLUENCE OF CHARLES BULFINCH

WENTWORTH MEETING-HOUSE

About the time that the church on Corser Hill was completed a fire in Wentworth destroyed the town's meeting-house. Since towns no longer were permitted to tax their citizens to build houses of worship and no denomination in Wentworth was ready to provide a building, the problem was solved in a most unique manner. The men of Wentworth organized a Meeting-House Association which issued three thousand dollars worth of stock to which everybody subscribed according to his financial ability. Today the church is said to "belong to everybody" and everybody worships there. Ministers of various denominations have filled its pulpit as pastors for the entire town.

Here was the last masterpiece of colonial workmanship in wood. A broad based fan-blind in the north gable and dentil corbels at the eaves embellish the walls. The steeple has two stories with a domed top like those at Newbury and Webster. Hand carved patterns form a frieze beneath the copings of each story and elaborate balustrades with urns at the corners outline the three sections. This steeple completes the influence of Charles Bulfinch in Northern New Hampshire.

Before a disastrous fire swept through the village about fifteen years ago, stately colonial homesteads surrounded the triangular village green, each an example of the country builder's art. Several escaped the flames, among them the Whipple residence whose doorway is sometimes included among collections of the colonial doorways of New England.

Scattered in all parts of New Hampshire are churches built of wood that are approximately a century in age, probably one hundred or more in number, and each has beauty in its design. But these are not meeting-houses and do not belong in this story. Canterbury, Francestown, Keene, Bedford, Dunbarton, Milford and many others are architecturally worthy of description. Their builders followed the designs of Bulfinch and ther Benjamin. In Keene the Congregational Society erected the First ch in 1825 with a stee design that was copied from Fitzwilliam. 1860 decade, the Corinthian order superseded the colonial simplicity original portico and steeple.

The Unitarian Church at Peterborough by Charles Bulfinch - 1827

The Ancient Foot-scrapers

The brick work of the church in Peterborough is laid in Flemish bond. Sir Christopher Wren always employed this method.

THE BULFINCH CHURCH AT PETERBOROUGH

Three brick buildings complete the story of colonial architecture in New Hampshire.

The one design by Charles Bulfinch is in Peterborough. In the biography, "Charles Bulfinch, Architect and Citizen" by Rev. Charles A. Place of Lancaster, Massachusetts, the statement is printed that, "There is a strong tradition amounting to a conviction" that the church at Peterborough was erected from plans that were actually drawn by Bulfinch. Although no record can be found that the plans were purchased directly from the architect, yet Judge Jonathan Smith, a native son of Peterborough, vouched that his father told him he assisted in their purchase in Boston after they had been rejected by another church in Massachusetts. In Lancaster, Massachusetts, the story is believed that in 1816 the church committee inspected the Peterborough plans but

The Wine-glass Pulpit

did not find their size adequate to their demands. Since many of the designs that Bulfinch sold do not appear in his recorded lists there is not a shadow of doubt that Judge Smith, who was twenty-two years of age at the time, learned the facts from his father.

Every evidence of the distinguishing motives of a Bulfinch building are found here. The recessed panels in the walls, the fan-blind in the gable and the three arched doorways are the prominent characteristics of this master. The steeple is a complete departure from previous designs in the state with the clock placed above the belfry, with curved mouldings about its face and the varying heights of the several stories, possibly inspired by the spire of St. Mary le Strand by James Gibbs in London. As a rule, Charles Bulfinch did not design tapering spires. One exception is that on Christ's church in Boston, known familiarly as the "Old North" of Paul Revere fame, but there he was reproducing a previous steeple that had been destroyed in a gale. The Lancaster, Massachusetts steeple—said to have been evolved from that at St. Mary le Bow in London, and considered to be the most beautiful that Sir Christopher Wren built in that city—is regarded by many architects as Bulfinch's masterpiece in church architecture.

Several years ago the chancel at Peterborough was remodeled to include a wine-glass pulpit, the only design of this type in the state, a reminder of King's Chapel in Boston.

THE NEWPORT CHURCH

Another brick church in Newport combines a Bulfinch building with a wooden steeple that was evidently copied from Acworth in 1828. The plans were drawn, we were told, from pattern books by local builders. A recent remodeling has removed many of the features of the Bulfinch interior, yet the characteristic horseshoe curve of the parapet of the balcony is retained with the same corbeled frieze motives that appear in all of this architect's designs. Two circular, fluted pillars support the ceiling in the choir, also distinctions of this famous man's genius. The entire edifice is an excellent specimen of colonial architecture at the culmination of craftsmanship of country carpenters in New Hampshire.

The Congregational Church at Newport
1828

THE CONGREGATIONAL CHURCH
AT NEWPORT

The distinctive marks of Bulfinch appear in
the brick work and doorways and those of Elias
Carter and the unknown architect at Acworth in
the steeple.   Unfortunately, the record of the names
of the artistic carvers that displayed their genius
in the cornice and steeple are forgotten.

The Congregational Church at Dover
1825

THE INFLUENCE OF CHARLES BULFINCH

DOVER'S CONGREGATIONAL CHURCH

As a last word, the end of our trail finishes where ecclesiastical history began in the state, at Dover. From 1633 to 1825 are two centuries of progress and the contrast of that little log hut with the present brick church is vivid.

James Davis, architect and superintendent of construction of the foundation and walls, must have studied the design of the State House in Boston erected by Bulfinch in 1795, for here are the recessed panels and the corbel or "crow-steps" above the gable which Bulfinch introduced into New England.

The windows, doors, and steeple were the work of George Pendexter and Samuel Drew. Evidently these men copied the pattern of their steeple from the upper members of Wren's St. Bride's near Fleet Street in London in many of its details, producing one of the most artistic spires in New Hampshire.

The interior woodwork, including the floors and the pews was the task of William Palmer and Joseph Pendexter. Joseph Babb copied the pulpit from another in New Haven, Connecticut.

The church in Dover is an excellent example of the combination of the designs of many previous creators which evolved into the colonial architecture of New England a century ago. Also the collective skill of various craftsmen was employed to produce a complete structure. Specialists in framing the walls and roofs, in the engineering of stairways, in carving interior finishing or decorative doorways or classic capitals for pilasters and columns, and masons and glaziers developed their individual handicraft and traveled from town to town, each contributing his particular skill to the structure. A building of a century ago was an aggregate of the arts assembled by the dexterity of experts in particular trades. Fortunately the records of the brick church in Dover contain the names of the men who displayed their ability before the days of machine-made products. Their accomplishments are the heritage of one of the first townships to be established in New Hampshire. Here the genius of old England and New England have combined to produce an architectural achievement of a high order.

229

The Unitarian Church at Nashua

THE INFLUENCE OF CHARLES BULFINCH

As the colonial period was ending and the Greek revival beginning about 1830, a new Unitarian church was built in Nashua, the first of the Greek type in the state. Mention is made of this church in this collection because its site is historic. Many years ago, on the bank of the Nashua River where Depot Square now hums with city traffic, the meeting-house lot was established for the settlement that is today called "The Gate City."

The Doric pillars of the portico are the guardians of the early cemetery in the rear of the church where, unknown to the thousands who hurry by, sleep the founders of the city on the slope of meeting-house hill close to the Daniel Webster highway. On the west side of this same hill rise the granite walls of the Congregational church, silently testifying to religious controversies that waxed and waned a century ago over doctrinal points in the religious convenants that separated the Puritans in New England.

JOURNEY'S END

Five years passed between the visit to Sandown and the last trip to Maine in the quest for colonial meeting-houses. The search extended far beyond any expectations in the beginning; the miles increased to many thousand; the discoveries proved enticing, each beckoned to more distant goals.

The meeting-houses of New England are a legacy from the Puritan ancestors reminding the living of
"The faith of our fathers, living still "
incarnate in the white oak timbers that were hewn by their vigorous hands; artistic and tangible in their handicraft in white pine; and immortal in the creative spirit that bequeathed to their children the designs of the colonial meeting-houses.

ACKNOWLEDGMENTS

The author gratefully acknowledges the assistance of Mrs. Harold A. Webster of Holderness who acted as chauffeur on all our trips; of Mr. George G. Clark of Plymouth, the photographer and for the use of his library. She wishes to express her appreciation for the loan of books from Mr. Edward Winslow Warren of Orford, New Hampshire, from Dr. Kan-Ichi Asakawa of the Department of History, Yale University, from Mr. Harold A. Webster of Holderness, New Hampshire, and for the cooperation of the entire staff of the library of the State Historical Society. She is deeply indebted to Russell F. Whitehead of New York for his courtesy which permitted the use of his plates from "The White Pine Series; Country Meeting-houses Along the Massachusetts and New Hampshire Line."

Letters from:

Augusta Nichols	Hampstead
Abbie A. Day	Jaffrey
Albert Annent (since deceased)	Jaffrey
Ruby B. Carter, Mrs. N. P. Ames	Chicopee Falls, Mass.
Mrs. Annie B. Shepard	Derry
Harriett Chase Newell	Derry Village
Clarence H. Walker	Alna, Maine
Karl G. Upton	Hancock
Arthur R. Webster	Milford
Lawrence Goodspeed	Boston and Stoddard
Mabel M. Boynton	Newcastle
Amy J. Dolloff	New Hampton
Mrs. Clifford Fifield	Lancaster, Mass.
Mrs. Howard M. West	Fitzwilliam
Donald D. Tuttle	Concord
Mr. Rudolph Wakefield, architect formerly with the firm of Coolidge, Bulfinch, Shapleigh, and Abbott	Boston, Mass.

BIBLIOGRAPHY

American Architecture —Fiske Kimball

The Architecture of Colonial America —Harold Donaldson Eberlein

Asher Benjamin —Aymar Embury II, Editor

Charles Bulfinch, Architect and Citizen —Rev. Charles A. Place

Connecticut Trilogy —Marguerite Allis

Early American Inns and Taverns —Elsie Lathrop

Early Domestic Architecture —F. Frederick Kelley

Elias Carter, Architect —Hárriette M. Forbes

Every Day Life in the Massachusetts
Bay Colony —George Francis Dow

The Granite Monthly, complete files

The Greek Revival —Howard Major

Historic Churches of America —Nellie Urner Wallington

The Homes of the Pilgrim Fathers
in England and America —Martin S. Briggs

London —Sidney Dark

Native Ministry of New Hampshire —Rev. N. F. Carter

New Hampshire Churches —Robert F. Lawrence

Old Churches and Meeting-houses in
and Around Philadelphia —John T. Faris

Some Old-time Meeting-houses of the
Connecticut Valley —Rev. Charles Albert Wight

Old New England Churches —Dolores Bacon

Paul Revere Bells —A. H. Nichols

Old Time New England Magazine —F. Frederick Kelley

Several Religious Societies in Portsmouth —Timothy Alden

Sir Christopher Wren, His Life and Works —Hodder and Stoughton, London

Three Old Maine Meeting-houses —Mrs. Horatio A. Duncan, Bath, Me.

The White Pine Series —Hobart B. Upjohn

Town Records of Fitzwilliam —Lewis M. Webb, Selectman

Genealogies of the Palmer, Spofford,
Stratton, and Clifford Families —Genealogical Library, Boston

Census of 1790 —New Hampshire Historical Society,
Concord

County Gazeteers of New Hampshire

Histories of All the Towns of New Hamp-
shire Where Meeting-houses Are —Library of New Hampshire Histori-
Situated cal Society

INDEX

Acworth, 139-143
Adams Female Academy, 104
Adams, Rev. Joseph, 52, 61
Alexander Studio, 4
Allenstown, 41-43
Alna, Maine, 201-202
Amherst, 23-33, 95, 183
Annett, Albert, 121-122
Ashby, Mass., 110, 118
Athol, Mass., 117
Auction of Pews, 30
Avon, Conn., 187

Babb, Joseph, 229
Babson, Major, 73
Barcas, William Elisha, 119
Barker, Francisco W., 69
Barnstead Parade, 61-64
Bartlett, Dr. Josiah, 21, 87
Basket, John, 159
Battle of Bunker Hill, 121
Belknap, Rev. Jeremy, 50
Benjamin, Asher, 109
Blake Bell Co., 97, 120
Bradford, 85
Bridgewater Hill, 47
Brooklyn, Conn., 95, 183
Browne, Rev. Arthur, 159-168
Brown, Gawen, 95
Bulfinch, Charles, 109, 211
Bunker, Eli, 61
Buntin Chapter, D. A. R., 41

Campton, 95
Canaan Street, 82-83
Cann of Jaffrey, 122
Canterbury, 23, 180
Carleton, Joseph, 201
Carter, Elias, 116-117
Center Church on the Green, 90
Church of England, 25, 159
Clifford, Ebenezer, 57-58

Colby, Peter, 7
Conant, John, 122
Concord Second Church, xvi
Connecticut, 181
Cornish Street, 166
Corser Hill, 55, 214-219
Crucifixion Doors, 11, 130
Cummings, Carpenter, 76

Dana Hill Church, 45-47
Dana, Dr. Simeon, 45
Davis, James, 229
Day, Abbie A., 122
Dedication Day, 31
Downing, Col. John, 52
Dover Congregational, 228-229
Dover Point, 49
Drake's Corner, 69
Drake, Weare, 69
Drew, Samuel, 229
Dunbarton, 32, 221

Eagle Hall, Milford, 97
East Derry, 5, 101
East Haven, Conn., 187
Effingham, 68
Evans, Rufus, 63
Exeter, 55-57

Farmington, Conn., 91, 95, 184
Feathered Clapboards, 9
Fitzwilliam, 112-120
Flemish Bond Bricks, 185, 223
Fort Meeting-house, 50
Framing the Meeting-house, 26
Fremont, 37-38

Gibbons, Grinling, 185
Gibbs, James, 108
Gibson, Sir Richard, 159
Gilman, Jotham, 44
Gilmanton, 44-45
Glazing, 29

Gordon Family, 47
Greek Revival, 188, 230
Greenland, 57

Hampstead, 98-101, 136
Hancock, 130, 132
Harvey, John Carpenter, 83
Haven's Hill, Rochester, 48
Hawke, 35-37
Hebron, 88
Henniker, 74
Hidden, Samuel, 70
Hill Center, 87
Hillsborough, 75
Hingham, 92
Hodgdon, Benjamin, 63
Holbrook Bell Co., 97
Holderness, 168-173
Hooper, Henry N. & Co., 104,
    120, 122
Hopkinton, 71
Hubbard, Benjamin, 118
Huse, Thomas, 99
Huston, George A. 203-204

Isles of Shoals, 178-179

Jaffrey Town-house, 120-129
Jones, Inigo, 103, 106

Kendall, Sally, 119
Kearsarge, Mount, 88, 217
Kelley, Rev. John, 100
King Post Truss, 28, 127, 164, 203
King's Town, 35, 86

Lancaster, Mass., 209, 212
Lawful Money, 3, 25
Lear, Tobias, 160
Leighton's Corner, 64-65
Lempster, 79
Lincoln, President Abraham, 58
Livermore, Samuel, 168-170
Locked Joints, 20-21, 205
Lord's Hill, 69
Lyon, Mary, 104
Lyme, 157-158

MacDowell Colony, 4
Magoon, Stephen S., 47
Main, Rev. Amos, 48
Meeting-house Hill, 3
Milford Town-house, 96
Minister's Lot, 3
Monadnock View, Jaffrey, 128
Morrison, Joseph, 103
Mount Ascutney, 163, 166
Mudgett, Benjamin, 44

Nashua, 230-231
Newbury, 103, 210-213
Newcastle Church, 60
New Hampton, 47
New Haven, 90
Newport, R. I., 208
Newport, N. H., 226-227
Nichols, Perkins, 96
North Danville, 35
North Hampton, 97-191
North Meeting-house, Portsmouth,
    59
Nutter, Benjamin, 63

Oldest Pulpit, 36
Oldest Meeting-house, 51
Old North Steeple, 94, 146
Old South Steeple, 94-95
Ordination Rock, 70

Palladio, 103-105
Palladian Windows, 134, 139
Palmer, Timothy, 58, 121, 191
Park Hill, 148-154
Patrick, Joel, 125
Peterborough, 222-223
Pendexter, George, 229
Piper District, 67
Place, Rev. Charles A., 224
Plymouth, N. H., 194
Poplin, 35
Porter, Noah, Jr., 91
Puritan Steeple, 92, 136

Quakers, 174-175

237

Queen Caroline, 158
Queen's Chapel, 159

Rand, Deacon Hiram, 61
Reed, Col. Thomas, 99
Reynolds, Deacon Daniel, 103
Rindge, 144-147
Rochester, 48
Rockingham, Vt., 199
Rocky Hill, 190-195
Rogers, Abner, 99

Sacred Desk, 16
Salisbury, Mass., 191
Salisbury, N. H., 85
Sandown, 7-21
Sandwich, 87
Searle's Hill, 85
Seat of Honor, 18
Shakers, 180
Shapleigh, Major, 175
Shaw, Thomas R., 7, 9
Sheffield, Mass., 196
Ship Church, Hingham, 92-93
Sinclair, Richard, 64
Smith Meeting-house, 44-45
Spofford, Daniel; Jeremiah;
    Jacob, 121, 191
Springfield, Mass., 189
St. Bride's, London, 67, 107
St. John's, Portsmouth, 158
St. Martin in the Field, 108
St. Mary le Bow, 107
Stoddard, 78
Storrow Town, 87
Stratton, Thomas, 117-118

Sutton, North, 81

Tabor, Church; Joseph, 77
Tamworth, 70
Templeton, Mass., 111, 118
Theological Seminary, 44
Toleration Act, 1
Town Pound, Sandown, 8
Town Horse Block, 53-54

Union, 67
Upping Stone, 177

Vinegar Bible, 159

Wakefield, 66-67
Waldoboro, Maine, 206
Walker, Clarence, 201
Walpole, Maine, 203-206
Ward, Rev. Jonathan, 203
Washington, Conn., 182
Washington, N. H., 75-77
Webb, Lewis, 118
Webster, 214-219
Webster, Col. David, 29; Capt.
    John, 87; Ebenezer, 87
Wentworth, 220-221
Wethersfield, Conn., 185
West, Mrs. Howard M., 117
West Claremont, 161-165
Wheeler, Dr. John, 61
Windsor, Conn., 188
Windsor, Vt., 201
Witch Doors, 11
Wren, Sir Christopher, 67,
    106-107

Young, Jonathan, 63